SECRETS OF SUCCESS FROM THE STORY OF BILL GATES

THE STORY OF BILL GATES – It is possible!

Lyton Chandomba

Raising Champions. London.
Champions Club is an imprint of LCMM

Copyright

Table of Contents

ACKNOWLEDGMENTS 1

CHAPTER 1: INTRODUCTION 2

CHAPTER 2: MICROSOFT IS BORN 7

CHAPTER 3: GLOBAL INFLUENCE 10

CHAPTER 4: SUCCESS COMES WITH A GREAT VISION 12

CHAPTER 5: SUCCESS STARTS IN THE MIND 19

CHAPTER 6: STRATEGIC THINKING 26

CHAPTER 7: MAKE THE MOST OF EVERY OPPORTUNITY 29

CHAPTER 8: MEETING PEOPLE'S NEEDS 32

CHAPTER 9: LAW OF PERSISTENCE 35

CHAPTER 10: CREATIVE IDEAS 52

CHAPTER 11: VALUE PEOPLE 57

CHAPTER 12: SHARE YOUR VISION WITH YOUR TEAM 59

CHAPTER 13: THE WISDOM OF FAILURE 62

CHAPTER 14: LEARN FROM YOUR CUSTOMERS 70

CHAPTER 15: TAKING ACTION TO CREATE RESULTS 74

CHAPTER 16: LOOK AT THE BIG PICTURE 79

CHAPTER 17: GIVE BACK 83

CHAPTER 18: WORK SMART 86

CHAPTER 19: FOLLOW YOUR PASSION 89

CHAPTER 20: LEAVE A TRAIL 93

CHAPTER 21: LIVE YOUR VALUES 96

CHAPTER 22: SURROUND YOURSELF WITH THE RIGHT PEOPLE 99

CHAPTER 23: INNOVATION IS THE HEART AND SOUL OF A BUSINESS............ 102

CHAPTER 24: MAKING MAXIMUM IMPACT AND CHANGING THE WORLD..... 105

CHAPTER 25: CONCLUSION 108

BIBLIOGRAPHY... 111

ABOUT THE AUTHOR 116

ACKNOWLEDGMENTS

I would like to thank Bill Gates he has been an inspiration to me and contributed to my thinking. Bill Gates is a visionary, pioneer and strategic thinker. He is one of the most influential people of our times. He has changed our world and the postmodern era.

CHAPTER 1: INTRODUCTION

In school he bragged to his teachers that he would be a millionaire by the time he was 30; he told his professors at Harvard that he would be a millionaire by the age of 30. He became a billionaire at 31. Bill Gates had a vision of starting his own company since he was a child. He 'planned' to form a company. At the same time, both Bill Gates and Paul Allen had a vision that there would come a day when 'everyone' would have personal computer. In those days, the size of an average computer was about the size of an average room. Imagining that everyone would have a computer one day was something others laughed at.

William Henry Gates III

William Henry Gates III is an American business mogul, magnate, tech visionary and business trailblazer, philanthropist – from 2009, the world's richest person. He is the founder and chairman of the software company Microsoft™, which he founded with his school friend Paul Allen. Bill Gates built Microsoft from scratch – he created the single most influential technology company of our modern age, and it made him so wealthy that he is now able to focus on the eradication of poverty and disease through the work of his charity foundation. The miracle of Microsoft is that Windows software is on almost every personal computer in the world. He turned Microsoft into a software behemoth that shaped the digital lives of hundreds of millions of people around the world and led it to dizzying success. He began his career at Microsoft in 1975 as the Chief Executive Officer and Chief Software Architect, a position he created. He is the largest individual shareholder with more than 4.5 percent common share stock. Bill Gates has also co-authored two books – The Road Ahead and Business @ the Speed of Thought.

His early childhood

William Henry Gates III was born in Seattle, Washington, to William Gates, Sr. and Mary Maxwell Gates. The Gates family did not realise that their first-born child was going to change the face of the world with computing technology. His family had a good track record in business, politics and community service. The diligence and dedication of the young man indicated that he was going to surpass all of his family in terms of intelligence and competitive spirit. Early on, his parents had a career in the law in mind for him. He was very bright in school from the very onset, particularly in science and mathematics. His parents moved him to a private school which is where he was introduced to the world of computers.

First Encounter with Computers

In spring 1968 the Lakeside School decided to obtain computers for their young students. Back then computers were expensive, so they fundraised and bought computer time from General Electric. The young men of Lakeside School soon became computer addicts!

There is one thing all successful people have in common. They will not be denied their destiny. They refuse to give up until they win. Gates instantly became inseparable from the new gadget, the computer. The computer room became his second home. He would stay in there all day and night, researching, reading anything about computers and writing programs. He was hungry for computers. You have to be hungry for whatever you are doing if you are going to succeed. Gates started to run into problems with the school authorities because he was spending most of his time in the computer room while his homework was left untouched. To make things worse, all the time bought from GE was used up within a matter of weeks.

Later in 1968 a new organisation opened for business in Seattle, the Computer Centre Corporation (CCC). The school struck a deal with CCC that allowed their ambitious young student Bill Gates to continue to access computers. Gates and his friends began exploring the inside of this new gadget. Within a short time the young men broke it down, exposing its weaknesses, changing files and systems. The students were so hungry for computers that they tampered with the file that recorded the amount of computer time they were using. CCC discovered this and banished them from using the system for some time.

The young men founded a computer club to further their goal of becoming computer gurus and also to get the opportunity to apply their new learned skills in the real world of computers. Their banishment from the Computer Centre was a temporary setback. Their roguish behaviour was a blessing in disguise. The Computer Centre Corporation's business was starting to dwindle as a result of weak systems security which meant that the system often crashed. The owners of the organisation were astonished by the intelligence of the students. They wondered how they had managed to alter and reconfigure their files. They were impressed with Gates and the other Lakeside computer addicts' show of intelligence and ambition. The Computer Centre realised that the solution to the major setbacks in their business might be found in these unscrupulous young men and they decided to hire them. Their job description was to expose bugs and weaknesses in the computer system, in return for which they would be allowed unlimited computer time.

Gates and his friends were involved with the computers day and night, constantly learning. It is true that specialisation, focusing on one particular thing, brings better results. As long as you maintain that focus, you will see results. It was here that Gates and Allen began to develop the talents that would lead to the formation of Microsoft seven years later. Gates developed his belief that in the 21st century the computer would be an invaluable device on every office desktop and in every home.. With his friend Allen, he began to work on software creation for personal computers. Gates' insight and his vision for personal computing have been essential to the success of his organisation, and the whole software business.

Roots of Gates' business career

In 1969 the Computer Centre encountered financial difficulties that led to it shutting up shop in March 1970. The young men of the Lakeside Programmers Group had to look for a new way to get computer time. Science Inc. hired them to prepare a payroll program. This brought the young men free computer time and income. Now they had to be registered and become a legal business. Science Inc. agreed to pay them royalties whenever they sold their programs. Gates and Allen's next computing project was the Traf-O-Data company. This company produced a new computer which was used to measure the flow of traffic. This venture earned them a whopping $20,000 and ended when Gates opted to go to college, but it was not long before Gates and Allen began to get more computer opportunities. While Gates was at Harvard, they began to talk seriously about starting their own software company.

CHAPTER 2: MICROSOFT IS BORN

At Harvard, Bill Gates was set for a career in law. But his first year saw him spending more time in the computer lab than in class for his legal studies. Gates did not have a systematic study schedule – He could get by on just a few hours' sleep and used cramming methods to pass tests with merely average grades. He remained in contact with Paul Allen who dropped out of Washington State University and moved to Boston, Massachusetts, to work for Honeywell.

In December 1974, Allen went to visit his friend Gates. On his way he picked up a current issue of an electronics magazine and in that magazine he saw the world's first microcomputer, the Altair 8080. He brought the magazine to Bill and the two young men were excited about this breakthrough. Bill and Paul were fascinated with the possibilities that this computer offered to further their ambition toward personal computing. Immediately, they called the manufacturer of the Altair 8080. Gates advised the manufacturer that they had software that would run with their new computer. The manufacturers were excited and asked Gates to bring the programme for testing. The young men did not yet have the software they had promised – the call was to gauge the company's interest and see if they could get business from the company. They began to work on the software which they called BASIC. Gates and Allen realised that their opportunity had come. The program was presented to the company and it worked perfectly for the first time. A contract was struck with Allen and Gates retaining their rights to their BASIC software. The two were absolutely certain that the software market had just been born. They named their partnership Microsoft, blending the words micro-computer and software, set up their first office located in Albuquerque and Microsoft was registered. A new era had begun in the world of computers!

The Microsoft BASIC™ software became the 'in thing' with computer hobbyists, but only about ten percent of the people using BASIC in the Altair computer had actually paid for it and at that time people were only using the computer for interest sake and not for money. Gates had ascertained that a pre-market copy was being pirated and widely circulated in the computer community. Gates set out in a newsletter his belief that software developers should be paid for their software; he declared the free distribution of software tantamount to stealing, since it was created to be sold. Microsoft relocated from Albuquerque to its new home in Bellevue, Washington, in 1979. Microsoft received royalties and fees for the use of their BASIC software program in the Altair computer but they could not break even.

Through innovation and constant improvement in the computer industry Microsoft experienced tremendous growth, between 1978 and 1981, and within a short period of time staff increased from 25 to 128 and its revenue increased from $4 million to $16 million. With a global mindset, Microsoft opened offices in Japan and United Kingdom, and by then almost 30 percent of the world's computers were running Microsoft software.

In 1986, Microsoft took a new direction by launching as a public corporation. The initial shares were sold for $21 per share and Bill Gates instantly became a millionaire, at the age of 31. Within a year, the Microsoft stock had increased to $90.75 per share and Bill Gates was a billionaire. He is the largest individual shareholder with more than 4.5 percent common share stock. In 1999, when the stock levels were at all times high, Bill Gates' fortune was worth $101 billion.

In 2005, Gates stated that he had gone to work every day since 1975. In 2013, Microsoft revenue annual revenue was US$77.85 billion and the company employed more than 91,000 people in 103 countries.

CHAPTER 3: GLOBAL INFLUENCE

Bill Gates is one of the most influential people of our times. The shape of the world has been changed by this man of influence. The Microsoft Windows™ operating software is being used in almost all offices and homes all over the world. He has changed our society, the way we do business, the way we live our lives, almost everything. Bill Gates has made a global impact with his vision and foresight. Time magazine named him one of the 100 people who most influenced the 20th century and in 2001 The Guardian newspaper included Gates among the 'Top 100 influential people in the media'. You cannot stop a man with a vision.

He was number one on the Forbes list of the richest people in the world from 1995 until 2006. He has a sumptuous home, endowed with good gardens and an anthology of artefacts. In 1994, Gates and his wife Melinda founded a charitable organisation called the Bill and Melinda Gates Foundation which supports initiatives in global health and education. The aim of the foundation is to eradicate poverty, disease and illiteracy from the world.

Awards

Time magazine named Gates one of the 100 people who most influenced the 20th century, as well as one of the 100 most influential people of 2004, 2005 and 2006. Bill and Melinda Gates, with singer Bono, were named by Time magazine as the 2005 Persons of the Year for their humanitarian efforts.

Bill Gates has received numerous international and national accolades, and honorary doctorates from the Royal Institute of Technology, Stockholm, Sweden in 2002, Waseda University, Tokyo, Japan in 2005, Harvard University in June 2007, and other universities. He was also made an honorary Knight Commander of the Order of the British Empire (KBE) from Queen Elizabeth II in 2005.

CHAPTER 4: SUCCESS COMES WITH A GREAT VISION

Write the vision and engrave it so plainly upon tablets that everyone who passes may be able to read it easily and quickly as he hastens by. – Habakkuk 2:2 Amplified Bible

The most pathetic person in the world is someone who has sight, but has no vision. – Helen Keller

You must have a vision for your life. Bill Gates' vision was to develop a personal computer for every one. A computer on every desk and in every home. So, the first lesson: Think big, think different and put in all your effort to execute the vision. Don't limit your imagination; you may be the next creator of life-changing invention.

Vision can be defined as a mental picture or image of a possible and desirable future state of an individual or organisation. It is your billboard image of your future end result. John Maxwell, the leadership expert, in his observation over the last 20 years of working with effective leaders, found they all possessed one common element – they had a clear vision of what they want to accomplish. The vision becomes the compass that helps to navigate through obstacles encountered on the way to achieving the dream. Unity is vital for the vision to be achieved – when the leader's vision becomes contagious it sets the followers on fire, they are willing to work even longer hours, morale soars, time flies and everyone is committed and willing to go the extra mile to achieve the vision. 'Why? Because the Leader has a vision!' 'I think that the greatest gift God ever gave man is not the gift of sight but the gift of vision', Dr. Munroe said a vision is a direct function of the heart, while sight is a function of the eyes. When you don't have a vision you live by what you see with your optical eyes. Vision will give you direction, resilience, courage and persistence throughout challenging times.

Every leader has a vision. For Nelson Mandela, it was a South Africa without Apartheid. For Martin Luther King Jr., it was a society in which race was not an issue in how people were treated or how they lived their lives. For Susan B. Anthony, it was a United States in which women had the right to vote. For Bill Gates it was a computer on every desk and in every home.

On Vision

A leader should have an impeccable vision and should be able to see what might lie ahead in times to come. Bill Gates could 'see' that the future of computers was in the software, not in the hardware – making things easy for him as he now had well-defined targets to chase. According to Gates, most successful people have had a vision which has enabled them to make it out big in the world. A leader without a clear vision soon loses their team and goes out of the race. This mental image, or picture, of the future has the capacity to grow inside the mind of leader and becomes more and more vivid with time.

The basic guiding vision of Bill Gates was that every business and household must have a computer and must run Microsoft software. Both Bill Gates and Paul Allen had their vision at an early age – in those days, the size of a computer was about a room – even imagining that everyone will have a computer one day was something others just laughed at. When the world was unaware of the software industry's future, here was a man who trusted in his intuition and passion and decided to take his vision the farthest possible way. This clear vision won him several laurels and he went on to be the richest person in the world for 13 years. In the words of Praveen Sherman: 'Do what you are Passionate about, the rest will follow.'

It's one thing to be smart, it's another thing to be resourceful, it's yet another thing to get results. Bill Gates is a visionary who makes things happen by creating systems bigger than himself and inspiring people to join him on his epic adventures to make maximum impact on the World. A vision is a future state of being for an individual, a team, a department, an organisation, a community, a nation, or the World. It is an idea, a way of being, that captures the minds and hearts of people. If the leaders and their people don't know where to go, then leadership means nothing. So it is important for leaders to have a clear vision of the future destination of the organisation so the followers rally behind the leadership. Your vision is possible, as long as you take the necessary steps each day to bring yourself closer to the vision it will become a reality. As a leader, you have to help people to embrace your vision and make it their own. This is an important step in bringing people together to work towards a common goal. Members of a team or staff need to have a shared vision and a sense of ownership in order to be committed to the organisation. That is key in helping people stay with an organisation for the long haul.

When you don't have a vision for your life you wonder aimlessly through life going nowhere and you end up getting stuck. Vision will give you a sense of direction and purpose. True success can only be achieved by following your purpose in life. Motivation becomes strong when you have a vision, a clear mental image of what you want to achieve and a strong desire to accomplish it. In such a situation, motivation awakens inner strength and power and pushes you forward, toward making your vision a reality. It starts with having a clear vision of what you want to accomplish in life, which is the first step towards success. Most successful people start with a vision in mind; they begin by visualising the end result before the beginning in every venture. Visualise your company going global and making an impact all over the world, see your book being published; begin with the end in Mind. Having a vision is very important in achieving your goals and it can be taken a step further by visualising and seeing the life you want to live in advance.

Visualize your desired end result, stay focused on your goal, and you will achieve your dream.

Bill Gates has shown great leadership with Microsoft, and vision always comes back to leadership. Leadership is about taking people somewhere. People always look at the their leaders for direction and vision. Bill Gates' vision was compelling and his picture of the future was so clear that people around him could see it. The power of a picture works when you focus on what you want to create, not what you want to get rid of. The power of a picture works when you focus on the end result, not the process to achieve it. Bill Gates' vision was crystal clear – to develop a personal computer for everyone.

The initial step is to have a vision. When you have a dream or vision write it down, make it clear. Don't limit your imagination or envisioning, dream big. You can always adjust your vision to be in line with the realities of the situation and time. Thinking big makes you to think outside the box because if you were thinking small from the beginning this will limit your imagination and possibilities. Thinking big also makes you think about the longevity of your vision, which is always a good thing to do and your vision may end up impacting the whole world. You don't pay anything to dream big not even a penny, it's free. Your vision should be flexible enough so that you can change it as circumstances change. That doesn't mean that you give up your principles or your hopes about what is possible, but as you collect information and advance your thinking you should adjust your vision to keep it up to date.

Write down 100 things in your journal that you truly want to achieve in your life so you can put your energy and time into reaching these goals. Write each goal clearly with passion and detail, as if you had already achieved these things, an important part of achieving your goal or desire is believing that it has already happened. Often we get what we see or focus on, so focus on success and I assure you sooner or later you will be successful.

A leader has to lead and communicate the vision to followers; the most important aspect of leadership is winning people over to a vision of what things can be like. You need to organise, draw up an action plan and hit the road running. As you lead, you should be communicating your vision all the time. People look to leaders to inspire them and keep them on the right track. The more you are enthusiastic and clear about where you are going, the more likely it will be that people follow your lead. Don't underestimate the power of your ideas and words. You, as much as anyone, have what is takes to lead others and to help them envision a better future for the organisation. You have the capacity to achieve your vision.

If you're on a powerful cruise ship, you can't control the weather. You know your final destination, but you might need to shift course a bit to ride out a bad storm or avoid an iceberg. Vision gives you the courage to shift course in a way that keeps you in sight of your true destination. Vision is travelling through untraveled road, yet you have a picture of your final destination. Knowing where you are going and your final destination needs a clear vision. Vision can develop inspiration, motivation and can ignite unity among people for success and they can make their decisions on the basis of end results which are already in their mind because of the vision.

Organisations are based on teams, and dedicated teamwork is required to make things happen. People need a clear picture of a future that motivates and inspire them to become that future. Once you have a vision, tell people about it and use it to lead people. Sharing a vision is a vital part of a leader; a vision gives people a bigger picture of what the organisation can achieve. It helps people raise their expectations and hopes; it inspires them. When people are inspired, they are more likely to work on the vision. Great Vision will unite people together and it will bring success.

CHAPTER 5: SUCCESS STARTS IN THE MIND

If you want to reach a goal, you must 'see the reaching' in your own mind before you actually arrive at your goal. – Zig Ziglar

Visualise this thing that you want, see it, feel it, believe in it. Make your mental blue print, and begin to build. – Robert Collier

Bill Gates was always ready to win. In the words of Zig Ziglar you were born to win, but to be a winner, you must plan to win, prepare to win, and expect to win. Bill Gates' greatest asset was a positive mindset from the onset and an aggressive relentless nature that wouldn't allow him to give up, no matter how hard it could have been. Most successful people, throughout history, have this common thread – they would not give up, they were persistent until they achieved their goals.

Success can mean very different things to different people, and it can depend on what one is seeking in life. To an athlete it may mean getting the gold medal, to doctors success can mean saving a life, to a lawyer it may mean winning a case in court, to parents success can mean raising children with good moral values and to some it can mean a job promotion or acquiring wealth. It may actually depend on one's perspective of the life that one has. The Oxford Dictionary defines success as the accomplishment of an aim or purpose. In simple terms success is achieving a goal. To achieve a goal, a person usually has to work on his goals and believe in himself. Success itself is, and can be, a chief motivator. When you are successful in one project this can give you the motivation to achieve other projects. Success can also mean being the best at what you do.

Success starts in the mind. You have to believe, desire and expect to be successful before you can achieve success. Develop the right mindset and you are likely to be moving towards success. What you can conceive with your mind you can achieve. What many people don't realise is the amazing power of our mind. It will be very difficult to achieve success until you have seen it with the power of your imagination or mind. In the wise words of businessman William Clement Stone: 'All personal achievement starts in the mind of the individual. Your personal achievement starts in your mind. The first step is to know exactly what your problem, goal or desire is.' You have to watch and take care of your thoughts, beliefs and actions as they are the tools to achieving success. If you are always thinking that you do not have what it takes to accomplish your goals then you will never achieve your goals, because you are simply closed to opportunities coming your way. The power of the mind is amazing yet we often fill our minds with more negative thoughts than positive ones. In achieving your goals your mindset matters more than you think, when it is complimented by designed action; it begins in the mind. Aiden Wilson Tozer, an American Christian preacher and author, said: 'What we think about when we are free to think about what we will — that is what we are or will soon become.'

You are in control of your life. The power to change the course of your life is yours, it starts with the thoughts you think — the attitude you have towards life. If you approach life with a negative attitude you will not live a life you love, and success may not be able to come your way. Your thoughts are the most essential factor in creating the life you want, take charge of your thoughts and you are in charge of your world. I cannot simply wish and dream to become a software magnate, or a best-selling author or a world class business mogul, I must take action, work on it and develop it — without taking action it will be fantasy or wishful thinking.

The mind is the source of dreams and ideas before visible success, where all great endeavours begin. You must visualize what you want before you get it. You must have faith-filled thoughts that lead you into action. The thinking initiates the dream, but faith causes you to take that first, uncertain step. The Book of Life says 'Faith without action is dead', and I say dreams without corresponding action are just fantasies. You were meant for great and unique things which demand you to commit yourself to an action plan towards the achievement of your goals.

One step will always leads to another step. According to the laws of physics, which says if something is set in motion it wants to remain in motion. Paulo Coelho, the Brazilian lyricist and novelist said the following: 'When a person really desires something, all the universe conspires to help that person to realise their dream.' William Hutchison Murray, the Scottish mountaineer and writer, alludes to the same thing in his famous words: 'Until one is committed, there is hesitancy, the chance to draw back, always ineffectiveness. Concerning all acts of initiative (and creation), there is one elementary truth that ignorance of which kills countless ideas and splendid plans: that the moment one definitely commits oneself, then Providence moves too. All sorts of things occur to help one that would never otherwise have occurred. A whole stream of events issues from the decision, raising in one's favour all manner of unforeseen incidents and meetings and material assistance, which no man could have dreamed would have come his way. Whatever you can do, or dream you can do, begin it. Boldness has genius, power, and magic in it. Begin it now.'

When you have achieved you goals in your mind you can begin to work on those goals daily by putting into action a plan of how you are going to manifest your goals into reality. Napoleon Hills said in his Hallmark expressions: 'Whatever the mind of man can conceive and believe, it can achieve.' You can achieve your goals if you can act as if they have already happened. I believe visualisation is one of the most powerful tools you can use to achieve your goals. Today visualisation is a tool that is now being employed by many people, particularly athletes and celebrities, to achieve their dreams, goals and to improve their careers.

Russian scientists carried out studies on creative visualisation in sports which has now become famous, they made four comparisons of Olympic athletes in terms of their mental and physical training ratios:

The first group received 100 percent physical training.

The second group received 75 percent physical training and 25 percent mental training.

The third group received 50 percent mental training and 50 percent physical training.

The fourth group received 75 percent mental training with 25 percent physical training.

The fourth group had the best performance results, indicating that mental training or visualisation can have significant measurable effects on biological performance.

The Americans trained very hard for the Olympic Games but they could not match Russian gymnasts and the Russian gymnasts dominated the Olympic Games. The other nations soon discovered that the Russians used sports psychologists to help with mental training methods and that the Russian athletes spent a few hours each day visualising their routines with perfect twists, jumps and landings.

Some celebrities and sports personalities have endorsed the use of creative visualisation and claimed it had an important role in their success – including Will Smith, Tiger Woods, Anthony Robbins, and Jim Carey. In 2008 successful actor Will Smith said he used visualisation to overcome obstacles and challenges, in fact he visualised his success years before he became successful. Another good example is that of actor Jim Carrey, who wrote a cheque to himself in 1987 for the sum of 10 million dollars. He dated it 'Thanksgiving 1995' and added the notation, 'for acting services rendered'. When times were tough he would sit on a hill top near Hollywood and play mind movies – seeing himself as a famous Hollywood movie star. He would take his check out and read it again and again as a reminder of his goal. He eventually signed a movie deal for more than 10 million dollars after he had visualised it for years, the date that he landed this deal was identical to the one written on the cheque he kept in his pocket.

You have to make a conscious decision to change your mindset and act with a new mindset for success. If you combine the right mindset, strategy, consistency and doggedness it will eventually result in success whether at work or any other area of your life. Having the right mindset is a key element to success. Most successful people reached their success in their own unique way, but all of them have one thing in common – a positive mindset. While mindset is a key element to your success it could also be a key element to your failure. It's a matter of choice, you can choose to stick to an unsuccessful mindset or you can choose to adopt a successful mindset and succeed.

CHAPTER 6: STRATEGIC THINKING

We can't solve problems by using the same kind of thinking we used when we created them. – Albert Einstein

Rarely do we find men who willingly engage in hard, solid thinking. There is an almost universal quest for easy answers and half-baked solutions. Nothing pains some people more than having to think. – Martin Luther King

Bill Gates, through constant improvement and innovation, has made Microsoft™ unique in the market. Bill Gates is a strategic thinker, which combined with determination, relentless effort and focus helped Microsoft to leverage the true power of computers by creating world changing software, Windows™ for the personal computer. He changed the world and changed his world. Persistence breaks resistance. Gates' persistence paid off by inventing the most popular window to the internet, Internet Explorer™ and the Microsoft Office™ platform. Bill Gates is a university drop out who went on to create the most innovative company in the world, Microsoft. Bill Gates also said if you want to get ahead in business, think ahead.

Strategic thinking is the process of formulating ideas that can help a desired goal. The term strategy derives from the Greek word strategia, meaning 'generalship' and simply means a plan or a high level plan for attaining a particular goal. It's an idea, a style of thinking, which sets a course of action that promises a winning future position.

The goal may be to create a new product, solve a problem or succeed in implementing a useful project. Strategic thinking helps in both short and long term planning, setting goals and determining priorities, and identifying potential risks and opportunities. Strategic thinking also involves coming up with alternative effective strategies or business models that deliver customer value. A company needs to compete with its competition; it needs a strategy to compete. A strategy is more than a plan, as strategy implies competing by outsmarting your competitors and providing unique value to your customers. For effective strategic thinking you have to be able to see the big picture, initiate innovative ideas and be flexible to alternative solutions and methods in defining a vision of the desired future and creating further new strategic ideas, which will enable the organisation to 'out-think' its competitors – creating tomorrow's competitive advantages today.

It can be difficult to be strategic. But a strategic thinker is always searching for the unusual – something that is different – and is able to set suppositions aside, purposely looking at things from different perspectives and refusing the urge to let one decision dictate or forecast future decisions. A person who has strategic perspective creates lucidity out of complex and ostensibly disconnected details, they can feel the winds of change, sense points of conflict and opportunity and articulate in concrete and convincing terms how they can be addressed, they get to the heart of a problem and see the relationship between key elements.

You can develop your strategic thinking ability by working on the following:

- being genuinely curious about what is taking place in your organisation, industry or wider business environment;
- being flexible by trying new ideas and ways of doing things;
- focusing on the future of the organisation's operational conditions that may change in the coming years;
- being open to new opportunities that you may capitalise on in the future as well as any threats that maybe coming in the future;
- maintaining an open mind viewing challenges as opportunities and believing that success is possible;
- and having openness to new ideas from others and customers.

For example, Bill Gates saw the future opportunities presented by the Internet and then began to work on it. His company did the same thing with a graphic interface computer while everyone was excited by MS DOS^{TM}, a computer operating system without graphics, they began to look into the future – conducting seminars about it and also working on Windows, a computer for the future. Strategic thinking involves zooming out and looking beyond the picture you see from where you stand – open minds are essential for a viable strategic thinking.

CHAPTER 7: MAKE THE MOST OF EVERY OPPORTUNITY

You were born to win, but to be a winner, you must plan to win, prepare to win, and expect to win. – Zig Ziglar

One secret of success in life is for a man to be ready for his opportunity when it comes. – Benjamin Disraeli

At the age of 13 Bill Gates had the opportunity to access a computer at school, at that time young people of his age did not have access to a computer. He knew how to maximise his opportunities by committing his life and time to the understanding of computers and technology. As previously noted Bill immediately became inseparable from this new gadget – the computer room virtually became his second home as he would stay in the computer room all day and night, researching, reading anything about computers and writing programs.

Formal education is not the only way to achieve success or reach your goal. When the opportunity presented itself to Bill Gates he dropped out of Harvard after realising that he could immediately make an impact on the world scene by starting a software company to make the most of new technologies. He realised that sometimes opportunities come knocking for an only short window of time, and one must seize that opportunity or it will be forever lost.

Bill Gates and his friend, Paul Allen moved to New Mexico to work with a company named MITS which gave them an opportunity to write Microsoft Basic™ which opened the door to building their software writing skills. They also capitalised on the opportunity presented to them by computer giant IBM. In the words of the Italian writer Niccolo Machiavelli: 'Entrepreneurs are simply those who understand that there is little difference between obstacle and opportunity and are able to turn both to their advantage.' Bill Gates is a visionary and entrepreneur who seized the opportunity presented to him by the invention of computers and made the most of it, becoming wealthy at a young age. Bill Gates is a world changer and a game changer who has used the opportunity presented to him by life to change his world and the world at large. In the words of Ben Sweetland: 'The world is full of abundance and opportunity, but far too many people come to the fountain of life with a sieve instead of a tank car ... a teaspoon instead of a steam shovel. They expect little and as a result they get little.' The truth is that the world is full of opportunities but many people don't capitalise on their opportunities because they sometimes look like too much hard work. Sometimes opportunity presents itself but people don't expect much from the opportunity, and therefore receive too little. You have to increase your capacity in order to take advantage of the opportunity presented to you. Bill Gates' vision was to put a computer on every desk and in every home, he could have only thought of creating software just for his home and his family. You must learn to think big so you can seize your opportunities in a big way. Bill Gates had the following to say on capacity when he was talking about General Motors: 'If GM had kept up with technology like the computer industry has, we would all be driving $25 dollars cars that got 1,000 MPG.' Bill Gates made sure the vision of a computer for every desk and every home was realised by constantly improving software and driving the prices of software and computers down.

Steven Snyder who joined Microsoft in 1983 as a Business unit Manager said Bill Gates 'opened a door for me in the 1980s and continues to be an inspiration even today'. He said the exceptional quality of Bill Gates is that he's a visionary who always looked continually towards the future, spotting opportunities and avoiding problems before they happened – spotting opportunities is an art that Bill Gates excels in.

CHAPTER 8: MEETING PEOPLE'S NEEDS

You can have everything in life you want, if you will just help other people get what they want. – Zig Ziglar

Successful people are simple problem solvers. – Mike Murdock

Don't be motivated by money but to meet people's needs and eventually life will reward you for your efforts – money is not the real motivator. Gates left Harvard without a guaranteed income in his new venture. He pursued his dream of developing software for a new world of information usage that satisfied his passion and stimulated his mind into a path of uncharted waters. Gates did not pursue money, money came to him because he offered the world something of great value – when you pursue your dream it is most likely that money will follow the value you add to society.

Making millions through programming was not his set goal; Gates was just following his heart, his passion. Programming was his obsession and it gave him happiness. When you make pursuing money your priority you may end up losing focus. Rather than just chasing the dollar sign, business starters and entrepreneurs should work hard to chase their passion; money will come on its own.

Bill Gates believed that people don't normally buy a product or a service due to its great logo or a low price or fame, but rather the product is a solution to their need, they buy because they are convinced the product is a solution to their need. The first and foremost important facet of marketing is to provide an unparalleled solution to an existing problem.

Zig Ziglar argues that when you buy a bed, what you really bought was a good night sleep. The bed was the solution to you need for sleep. So if you can solve that need people will buy your product because it's a solution. None of us buy products – we buy the products of the product, the benefits or need solutions, what the product does for us not what the product is. Helping others to get what they want is the true path to success.

When you solve someone's problem you will be rewarded for solving that problem. Bill Gates solved software problems through Microsoft and became wealthy in the process. Carl Benz solved the transportation problem by inventing the first modern car in 1886. Alexander Graham Bell was an eminent Scottish scientist, inventor, engineer and innovator who is credited with inventing the telephone and solving a communication problem. Thomas Edison solved the lighting problem by inventing the light bulb. When you go out to meet human needs you will eventually be rewarded for your efforts with success. According to Strive Masiyiwa, the Zimbabwean telecommunications mogul, meeting human needs is the most sure-fire way to succeed in business. Masiyiwa said: 'We didn't wake up and say we wanted to make billions of dollars; we said we wanted to extend telecommunications to all the people of Africa.' Identify and meet human needs on your way to success – this is what Bill Gates did, and he was rewarded with wealth in exchange. Think about an area that you are good at and go out and meet the needs of the society at large, you will surely be rewarded for your efforts. Let me sum up with the words of an American writer Orison Swett Marden: 'The golden opportunity you are seeking is in yourself. It is not in your environment; it is not in luck or chance; it is in yourself alone.'

CHAPTER 9: LAW OF PERSISTENCE

A river cuts through rock, not because of its power, but because of its persistence. – Jim Watkins

My success is based on persistence, not luck. – Estee Lauder

A highly significant business lesson from Microsoft Chairman and Founder Bill Gates is his doggedness and persistence. Success is not usually overnight. When he launched Windows 1.0™ the truth of the matter is that it wasn't much of a success but this did not change Gates' tenacity and determination. Was it the end of story? Certainly not! Microsoft released Windows 2.0™ two years later, in 1987, but it didn't fare much better. It found moderate success because of the software in particular, Excel, Word and Aldus PageMaker. When he launched the third version, in 1990, of the software with a graphical operating system it was an instant hit and the company sold over 10 million units of the software and it was a big money-maker, they received millions of dollars in profit in just two years. If Gates can do it, you can do it. We can learn business by reading good books, attending workshops and meeting good business people. Business is a mindset! According to Bill Gates, patience is a key element of success.

Persistence is defined as the 'the act of persisting or persevering ...' 'To continue steadfastly in pursuit of a mission'; 'dogged'; 'stubbornly unyielding'; 'dour determination'; 'continuing or repeating behaviour'; 'the sustained effort needed to produce belief'; 'will'. Persistence is also closely related to words like commitment as well as perseverance. The most successful people in life are always persistent. Persistent people are often accused of being cold and heartless, but a careful re-evaluation shows this is not the case at all, they are simply singled minded in their pursuit of their own personal destiny. This is why it is important to cultivate the quality of persistence, no matter what you are aiming for. Plant the seeds, the seeds being the idea, fertilise those thoughts with a burning desire and, through persistence, you will harvest your wildest dreams.

Persistence is the secret of success and it's a common feature around successful people. Calvin Coolidge 30th President of the United States wrote: 'Nothing in the world can take the place of persistence. Talent will not; nothing is more common than unsuccessful men with talent. Education will not; the world is full of educated derelicts. Persistence and determination alone are omnipotent. The slogan 'press on' has solved and always will solve the problems of the human race.'

You have to develop a tough skin and be relentless; life will sooner or later give its way. Nothing in the world can take the place of persistence; it will eventually break all resistance. You can overcome discouragement by pressing on and keeping on. When it seems that all your efforts towards success are not yielding anything you have to be relentless.

Jesus was describing the power of persistence when he declared: 'No man, having put his hand to the plow and looking back, is fit for the kingdom of God' (Luke 9:62). When you realize that prosperity is your divine heritage, you should persist in going after it. Pursue it tenaciously until you get it. 'Most failure is simply due to the fact that we take the line of least persistence' – Norman Vincent Peale. The Book of Life tells the story of Jacob wrestling with the angel until the break of day. This story shows the power of persistence in producing success. He vowed to the angel, 'I will not let thee go, except thou bless me' (Genesis 32:36). The angel renamed him 'Israel' which means Prince with God.

If you persist, you will prevail. Persistence requires a great deal of advance planning and premeditated thought. If you have been sidetracked and can't do anything directly to work toward it, there are little things you can do to get your vision back on your goal, and begin moving toward it in whatever way seems most logical at the moment. Never give up there is always a way out. Do what you are supposed to do; it will lead to bigger opportunities along the way. Just one step at a time, big or little, is all that is necessary – take it and it will lead to the next.

The persistent man also perseveres long enough for his dreams to catch up with him. Joyce Meyer said 'refuse to settle for anything less than everything God has for you'. If you can make up your mind that you will not settle for less, you will not settle for less. You will keep right on going and you will achieve your goals and dreams. If you convince yourself nothing is impossible, nothing will be impossible for you. When you get to a difficult place, keep on keeping on until you achieve your dreams. When you get to an unpaved road you will pave the way; when you reach the uncharted waters, you will chart the way forward. Don't concentrate on how hard it is but focus on the reward and satisfaction you get by achieving your goals.

Always focus on the final outcome from the start, never lose that ability to focus. As the road gets harder, you get harder; as the road gets tougher, you get tougher; as the journey becomes difficult and seems like it's impossible, just continue to focus and keep going and watch what will happen. The only true failure is when you give up and you stop moving on.

When problems are discovered, the persistent mind creates alternative routes and adjustable strategies. If the initial plan of action doesn't work, then a persistent thinker will have to come up with a new approach.

Persistent people make the world turn; they make business grow; they improve global communication and they help to shape this generation's zeitgeist. Why not become a part of this movement? Plan out your future and allow yourself the chance to become everything you aspire to be. Commit to your vision of success and help make the world a better place in your own unique way.

Persistence is something that you, and you alone, can control. You must have the drive to reach your goals otherwise without enough desire or reasons to achieve your goals you are more vulnerable to quit. When it comes to achieving your goals you must create new habits and they will guide towards achieving your goals, when they become involuntarily habits towards achieving your goals it will be easier to live and breathe your goals. Make sure you evaluate your progress on the road to your goals or results. When you see you are moving in the direction of your desired goals and you feel closer to reaching your goals this will boost your confidence levels and you will get excited about it – reward your progress when you reach a milestone.

There is always a way if you want more. Persistence and consistent action will make it happen. Thomas Edison had over 10,000 failed attempts to create the light bulb before he was successful. His invention was as valuable as his persistence. Many people would just simply give up after a few attempts – but look what he created after

10,000 failed attempts. You can change the world, or your world, if you are persistent enough. Make a resolution not to give up and maintain persistent, constant actions towards achieving your goals. Many business deals have been sealed when one of the parties has been persistent. Bring your best to every situation; you may never know when your breakthrough opportunity presents it to you. Persistence always pays off. Don't take rejections to heart or personally, it's only a normal process of taking out what is not good for you. Persistence takes action. There is always a way to achieve your goals, dreams and experience the life you truly desire. It is always too early to give up, never, never give up.

How badly do you want it? If you truly want to achieve it then nothing will stand in your path. You can only become persistent enough to succeed when your desire to reach your goal exceeds the pain you have to go through trying to achieve it. The pain of living without your dream should simply exceed the pain of paying the price to accomplish your goal. A burning desire to succeed will propel you to do whatever it takes to get it; you will become focused and persistent. The end result of this success is inevitable.

When you discover your purpose in life and follow it persistently, the end result is massive success. Persistent people help to change their generation; they make a contribution to the social and business world.

Plan out your future and fulfil your purpose. Make a commitment to follow your vision of success and help make the world a better place to live in your own different way. One of the main reasons why all successful people accomplish more than others is their dogged persistence. One percent of the population control 96 percent of the world's wealth. Have you ever wondered why is that way? Bill Gates has been persistent since he first encountered computers. It's good to pursue what you love to do the most and when you do what you love to do the most then it becomes easier to focus on something you love. When you love what you do you can be absorbed into it and persistence becomes easier.

You may encounter failure in your persistence. But failure is only another opportunity to begin again, only this time a little wiser than before. It's not how many times you have failed attempts that matters it's how many times that start a fresh attempt that matters. Without applying persistence you are doomed to fail before you even start. Things don't go wrong for you to make you frustrated, resentful, negative and give up – they happen to set you back and build you up, so that you can be all that you were intended to be.

Have You Heard of the Chinese Bamboo Tree Story?

In the first five years of a Chinese Bamboo Plant's life farmers consistently and faithfully water, fertilize, and nurture the tiny seedlings.

Year Number 1: No Visible Results.

Year Number 2: No Visible Results.

Year Number 3: No Visible Results.

Year Number 4: No Visible Results

Year Number 5: Typically, over about six weeks, the Chinese Bamboo Plant will soar to approximately ten storeys high!

Naturally, you might believe there is nothing going on for the first 5 years. To the contrary during that entire time, a strong and vast network of roots is developing beneath the earth's surface. These solid and sturdy roots will serve as a foundation capable of supporting the Chinese Bamboo Plant during its boundless, breakthrough moment. This serves to prove the point that just because we don't see immediate results doesn't necessarily mean there is no growth happening. Patience, persistence, and perseverance are often decisive elements for attaining success. Remember, if the farmer ever stops watering, fertilising, and nurturing the tiny seedlings at any time the Chinese Bamboo Plant cannot survive. The truth is, seeing the 'fruits of our labour' often takes the same amount of loyalty and commitment. Each step we take, each relationship we build, every new strategy we implement – all manage to intricately form the basis of our future achievements. Simply refuse to quit, many of life's failures are people who did not realise how close they were to success when they gave up.

Work on your thinking patterns because those thoughts are part of your inner self and they can help you to build a foundation for persistence. What we set our minds to we can accomplish, so success and its principles begins in our minds before we can see it. Habitual thinking, towards achieving your goals and subsequent actions based on your plans is the only thing that can bring you closer to your destiny. In the wise words of Louis Pasteur 'Chance favours the prepared mind'. It is the same with destiny, it usually gravitates towards people whose minds and hearts have been prepared and conditioned to become more persistent. You can start by setting your goals. It's been estimated that only 2 out of every 100 people have definite goals in life. It has also been widely accepted by experts who study people and success, that a lack of persistence is the major common cause of failure and the only trait most common among all people of the world. Apply persistence at all times until it becomes your daily habit.

Bjorn Rune Borg, former World number one tennis player from Sweden, said the following about persistence: 'My greatest point is my persistence. I never give up in a match. However down I am, I fight until the last ball. My list of matches shows that I have turned a great many so-called irretrievable defeats into victories.' There is no replacement for persistence. It cannot be substituted for any other quality or trait. When you face challenges above all else persistence will strengthen you in your journey. When you develop the habit of persistence you will be assured of reaching your destiny. No matter how many times you are defeated, hindered or faced with obstacles on your path, if you are persistent enough you will ultimately achieve your goals and reach your destiny. Persistent people seem to have an instinctive understanding that defeat is only temporary and will eventually turn into victory with enough tenacity.

Most people have settled for a life of mediocrity because they have surrendered to temporary defeat and setbacks. A few have reached their full potential by refusing to accept defeat and in the end they overcame all negative circumstances in their path to success.

Success is inevitable if you are passionate, having a burning desire and persistence to achieve your goals, not just a casual desire or wish.

Napoleon Hill wrote down what he believes are the four main steps vital for success in every walk of life:

1. A definite purpose accompanied by a burning desire for its fulfilment.
2. A definite plan explicit in continuous action.
3. A mind closed tightly against all negative and discouraging influences, including negative suggestions from relatives, friends, and acquaintances.
4. A friendly alliance with one or more persons who will encourage you to follow through with both plan and purpose.

A persistent strong desire pushes your goal into manifestation. Persistence conquers all. You may not have a giant leap towards success but little steps of persistence that will in the end lead to success. Persistence is the only attribute that separates those who have given up half way through and those who have succeeded. Determined and mentally strong people are sure to win their race and achieve their dream or the goal they have set for themselves, because of the spirit of persistence that prevails in their minds. To settle for failure to them is not an option, they merely see it as a stepping stone to success. They may encounter failure a number of times but it's their persistence that will ultimately take them towards success. Motivation ignites persistence and it can be motivation through words, actions and learning from those who have succeeded in the past. Education, hard work, talent, genius are all necessary ingredients to success but if persistence is not there these necessary ingredients will be of no help. Wishes and dreams can be converted into reality by having a burning desire and constant actions necessary towards achieving your goals. You can master all fear, discouragement and indifference if you are persistent.

When you master the art of persistence it will eventually dawn on you there is no mysterious secret to success. Centuries of study of the most successful people throughout history has not revealed any secret knowledge to their success. A careful study and examination of their life and actions revealed that they all possessed one common thread – an uncommon persistence, concentration of effort and determinateness of purpose.

There is no shortcut and no secret to true success, there is only a burning desire, complimented by a plan and followed through with constant action.

Wilma Pearl Mankiller, who was the first female chief of the Cherokee Nation, said the following: 'The secret of our success is that we never, never give up.' Sylvester Stallone, when he began as a young director, wrote a scenario but did not have enough money so went to a producer and showed him his outline of the movie but the producer told him that he was not qualified to be a director or a scenario writer. Despite the setback Stallone did not give up instead he went to a second producer who also told him that he was not talented. He went to five more different producers and for some reason they all said the same thing – that he was not talented and qualified as a scenario writer or director. What would you have done if it was you were in his shoes? You might have suffered from the rejections, simply given up, saying that life is not fair or you could have felt resentment and become negative about achieving your goals. Persistence will eventually break resistance; Sylvester Stallone persisted until he got 50 rejections from 50 different producers. On top of their rejections these experts in the film industry tried to convince him that he was heading for failure, that his case was hopeless and he would never make it in the film industry. Stallone believed in his dream and he was persistent so he refused to believe their negative words, as is mostly common with successful people, he went on to prove all those who rejected him and denied him the opportunity wrong. His idea was the first part of the Rocky series – which went on to be extremely successful. In the game of life you have to learn that persistence, rejection and success are part of life. You can learn from the Stallone story that rejections are never a proof that you are bad. There is no doubt that Rocky was a great scenario that Stallone was promoting, yet 50 different producers rejected it. Don't take rejection personally and don't buy into false illusion that rejection means you are incompetent.

Every successful person has been rejected once or even many times before they managed to became successful, it's only that we only usually see them in the limelight and often don't know people's stories.

If the rejections are coming from experts in the field it doesn't necessarily mean they are always right in fact all experts can be wrong. Some people can tolerate rejection if the source of rejections is their close friends, they are persistent enough to stand firm despite the rejections, but when they are told they are wrong by one or two experts their dreams would be instantly shattered. Sylvester Stallone was not rejected by 50 traffic wardens but he was rejected by fifty film producers who are the bright minds in the film industry nonetheless he went on to prove all of them wrong.

Thomas Carlyle, a Scottish philosopher and satirical writer, said the following about persistence: 'Permanence, perseverance and persistence in spite of all obstacles, discouragements, and impossibilities: It is this, that in all things distinguishes the strong soul from the weak.' Nothing on earth can stop a person who is persistent. For example if Stallone's Rocky scenario was bad and even if he was not talented he would have still succeeded, because of his resilience he would have worked hard on it until it became a great scenario. There is no force on earth that can prevent a person who is persistent in reaching his goals. You will accomplish goals if you are persistent enough. In summing up the difference between Sylvester Stallone and an ordinary person – it lies with persistence.

Another story of persistence and tenacity is that of Colonel Sanders, the founder of Kentucky Fried Chicken. At the age of 65 he was forced to shut down his restaurant business because a new highway was being built were his restaurant was located. Colonel Sanders had little to show for his life except a pension check of $105 and a chicken recipe. Instead of blaming the system, the government, the economy and society he began to think about a way out of the predicament he found himself in, he had a burning desire to change his circumstances. He began to ask himself life changing questions which changed the direction of his life. His questions were:

- What can I give back to other people?
- How can I add value to others?
- How can I make a difference?

He had a chicken recipe, and a plan to franchise this recipe to restaurants and make a living out of it. He took his recipe and got behind the wheel of his van, and made up his mind to make something of himself. His first plan was to sell his recipe to restaurant owners in exchange for 5 cents from their profit. The first attempt was a complete failure, the first restaurateur said his recipe was useless and they turned him down. The second attempt was a disaster they rejected his recipe saying that no one can ever taste it, the third attempt rejected him saying please throw your recipe in the bin. Rejection followed rejection, 1008 sales pitches were a complete disaster. Did Colonel Sanders give up? No he continued to call on new restaurant owners as he continued to travel across the United States of America. He had to sleep in his car so he could save money. Jesus gave us wise words of wisdom that persistence pays in the long run. The following words of Jesus said it all: 'And He said to them, Which of you who has a friend will go to him at midnight and will say to him, Friend, lend me three loaves of bread, For a friend of mine who is on a journey has just come, and I have nothing to put before him; And he from within will answer, Do not disturb me; the door is now closed, and my children are with me in bed; I cannot get up and supply you with anything? I tell you, although he will not get up and supply him anything because he is his friend, yet because of his shameless persistence and insistence he will get up and give him as much as he needs. So I say to you, Ask and keep on asking and it shall be given you; seek and keep on seeking and you shall find; knock and keep on knocking and the door shall be opened to you. For everyone who asks and keeps on asking receives; and he who seeks and keeps on seeking finds; and to him who knocks and keeps on knocking, the door shall be opened.' (Luke 11:5-10 Expanded Bible).

Restaurant owner number 1009 gave him his first 'yes' after his pitch – after two years of travelling without success his persistence paid off. He finally signed up five restaurants. He continued to press on believing he had a great chicken idea, which one day would become the best chicken in town. By 1963 Colonel Sanders' idea had caught on and he had 600 restaurants across the country selling his secret recipe of Kentucky Fried Chicken. He became a multi-millionaire in 1964 when he sold his business interests. Colonel Sanders teaches us that persistence will always lead to success if you are persistent enough. Nothing can stand in the way of someone who is persistent. Persistence helps an individual to break the negatives around him to achieve his dreams and goals. If Sylvester Stallone and Colonel Sanders can do it you can also do it. Nothing can stop you, in fact you are unstoppable. You will achieve your dreams or goals you will accomplish your purpose, you will reach your destiny.

CHAPTER 10: CREATIVE IDEAS

I think it's fair to say that personal computers have become the most empowering tool we've ever created. They're tools of communication, they're tools of creativity and they can be shaped by their user.' – Bill Gates

Everybody has a creative potential and from the moment you can express this creative potential, you can start changing the world. – Paulo Coelho

In the beginning computer screens were capable of just displaying text with no graphics such as the MS DOS™ system. Bill Gates and his friend Steve Ballmer predicted that the future of computers will be graphic interface operating systems and conducted seminars around the country about the future possibilities that lay in graphic interface operating systems. Sceptics and computer companies did not buy into their idea of graphic interfaces, they argued that it would be to slow and difficult to write graphic software. When windows announced in 1983 that they were putting their ideas to paper and developing Microsoft windows the computer companies were less amused. If you have a sudden life changing idea or paradigm shift don't worry if people don't get it. Start working on it now so that you will be prepared when the time is right.

The truth of the matter is that we are all creative beings; we were made in the image of the creator. What we have turned out to be is a product of what we have created. We can achieve our heart's desire and greatest potential by learning to tune into our creative ability. Albert Einstein approached his work as a form of joyous play with a childlike openness, audacity and with the ability to see ordinary things from different perspectives. Steve Job the co-founder of Apple Corporation said: 'Creativity is just connecting things. When you ask creative people how they did something, they feel a little guilty because they didn't really do it, they just saw something. It seemed obvious to them after a while. That's because they were able to connect experiences they've had and synthesise new things. To change your life and achieve your goals you have to be creative.'

According to the Oxford dictionary the term creative is defined as: 'relating to or involving the use of the imagination or original ideas to create something. It is used to describe originality of ideas or something that has not been previously thought of.' Creativity is defined by the business dictionary as the: 'mental characteristic that allows a person to think outside of the box, which results in innovation or different approaches to a particular task.' Creativity is the ability use your imagination to generate innovative new ideas and move them from thought realm into reality. George Bernard Shaw, an Irish playwright and a co-founder of the London School of Economics, said:

'Imagination is the beginning of creation. You imagine what you desire, you will what you imagine, and at last, you create what you will.' The meaning of creativity is being able to use your imagination and original thinking to come up with something unique and different. Edward de Bono, a Maltese physician, author, inventor and consultant who originated the term lateral thinking, said the following: 'Creativity involves breaking out of established patterns in order to look at things in a different way. It is better to have enough ideas for some of them to be wrong, than to be always right by having no ideas at all.' Creativity can be having the skills to invent something new, having the skills to come up with new methods to do something, having the ability to write creatively or even thinking up a new concept. Someone who is creative has a lot of imagination and new ideas. You are creative when you turn those new and imaginative ideas into reality.

You have to think outside the box to be creative. It involves new ways of thinking, bringing new solutions into existence and imagining new unique ways of doing things. It is pioneering a new path that previously didn't and, in the process, living a trail. To be creative you must forget any path you see, make your own path. While you have your clear cut goals you should be open to new possibilities, this will enhance your creativity. The postmodern world is changing, therefore creating new possibilities and new problems. You can discover new ideas and create possibilities and solutions for the postmodern world.

In the business world creativity is characterised by the ability to see the world in new ways, to make connections between seemingly unrelated phenomena, to find hidden patterns, and to generate solutions. Bringing forth fresh solutions to problems, and the ability to create new services, products and processes for a changing market, are part of the intellectual capital that gives an organisation its competitive edge. You don't need someone's permission to think and act, it's something that you can do with full control. You can take the initiative right now and try new things out. Don't be afraid of making mistakes, the fact is the more you try the more opportunities you will have to stumble on something new that will work and change your world and the world at large. Thomas Edison said: 'I make more mistakes than anyone else I know, and sooner or later, I patent most of them.'

Creativity is closely connected with innovation, while creativity involves two processes from thinking to production innovation is the implementation or production of an idea. Linda Naiman said the following: 'If you have ideas, but don't act on them, you are imaginative but not creative.' So creativity requires action, commitment and passion to bring something new into being. For creativity and innovation to flourish, corporations and organisations must create a conducive environment that nurtures creativity; putting together multi-talented people who work together – exchanging ideas and knowledge, and shaping the direction of the organisation for the future. Edward de Bono said the following on creativity as a great motivator: 'Creativity is a great motivator because it makes people interested in what they are doing. Creativity gives hope that there can be a worthwhile idea. Creativity gives the possibility of some sort of achievement to everyone. Creativity makes life more fun and more interesting.'

CHAPTER 11: VALUE PEOPLE

To add value to others, one must first value others. – John C. Maxwell

Always treat your employees exactly as you want them to treat your best customers. – Steven Covey

In order to be successful you must learn to value people and their contribution. Bill Gates had a grip on this principle and he paid his employees well and invested in their future. Most of the people he worked with have become wealthy through working for Gates. Gates is an effective communicator. He kept his employees motivated and encouraged to do their work with a positive outlook. Put the right information into the hands of the people so that they can make the most of it. Bill Gates said: 'The vision is really about empowering workers, giving them all the information about what's going on so they can do a lot more than they've done in the past.' The formula is, meet the needs of your employees and they will go out of their way to meet the needs of your customers or clients and your business will be more profitable. It's all about the first class service we give to people that will make a big difference to the business. In the competitive and complex business world people are often treated as commodities rather than being valued as human beings. You don't want to be an organisation that values customers only by what is in their wallets and have employees treated only as tools or machines for making profit for the organisation.

In the words of Anne M. Mulcahy: 'Employees who believe that management is concerned about them as a whole person – not just an employee – are more productive, more satisfied, more fulfilled. Satisfied employees mean satisfied customers, which leads to profitability. Employees are a company's greatest asset – they're your competitive advantage. You want to attract and retain the best; provide them with encouragement, stimulus, and make them feel that they are an integral part of the company's mission.' James Sinegal said: 'Paying your employees well is not only the right thing to do but it makes for good business.'

When you value your employees they will perform at their best providing their output for the organisation. You make the employees feel like they are your partners in business they feel valued and they will be the ambassadors of the company or the organisation.

CHAPTER 12: SHARE YOUR VISION WITH YOUR TEAM

Teamwork is the ability to work together toward a common vision. The ability to direct individual accomplishments toward organizational objectives. It is the fuel that allows common people to attain uncommon results. – Andrew Carnegie.

Talent wins games, but teamwork and intelligence wins championships. – Michael Jordan

As a visionary leader Gates saw the advent of the graphical interface years in advance, he predicted the pre-eminence of the Internet before the first dial-up connection was feasible.

In May 1995 Gates wrote a very long memo to his company staff regarding the coming of the internet, which he believed was the future for Microsoft and the company's survival and expansion plans. He ended by saying the following: 'The Internet is a tidal wave. It changes the rules. It is an incredible opportunity as well as incredible challenge. I am looking forward to your input on how we can improve our strategy to continue our track record of incredible success.'

Gates believed in sharing his vision with his team at Microsoft so that they were all on the same page. This finally paid off when Windows 95™ was launched, it was not only an operating software it came ready loaded with Internet Explorer™, which became one of the world's most popular internet browser.

Your vision for the organisation is like a billboard. It is a picture of your ideal organisation that puts across your ideas across powerfully, quickly and accurately. People will decide to follow you when they see a clear vision and are certain were you are heading. Sharing vision with your team is a vital role of a leader. A vision will give people direction and a bigger picture of what the organisation can be. The vision will inspire your team; it will help raise their expectations and hopes. When people are inspired they are more likely to work hard in order to achieve the vision of the organisation. Make sure you are communicating the vision of the organisation at all times. The more you do it the more you will get people rallying behind it in support and the better you will get at it. Jack Welch said: 'Good business leaders create a vision, articulate the vision, passionately own the vision, and relentlessly drive it to completion.'

If the vision is clearly communicated to your team often enough they will take ownership of the vision and they run with it. Successful people communicate their vision at every opportunity and they are always on the lookout for a chance to share their key message. In the words of Brian Tracy: 'Teamwork is so important that it is virtually impossible for you to reach the heights of your capabilities or make the money that you want without becoming very good at it.'

The leader always takes the lead; you should continue to communicate the vision and any modifications to the team at all times. People will look to you as the leader to be inspired and to keep them on the right track. The more you are passionate, relentless, showing great confidence and clear about where you are going, the more likely people will follow your lead.

Don't underestimate the power of your vision, ideas, dreams and words – you have what it takes to change your organisation and the world.

CHAPTER 13: THE WISDOM OF FAILURE

It's fine to celebrate success but it is more important to heed the lessons of failure. – Bill Gates

Every adversity, every failure, every heartache carries with it the seed on an equal or greater benefit. –Napoleon Hill

No one likes to accept they've failed. In life and in business people are many times remunerated and commended for their success. The down side of this is it creates a culture where people don't learn from failure, and thus will result in making the same mistakes. It's always good to celebrate success but it is more vital to pay attention to the lessons of failure. Bill Gates' approach that is great work and effort must be celebrated but mistakes should also be acknowledged and not swept under the carpet and must be worked upon until they become successes. As a result of mistakes Microsoft™ software has been hacked many times but they learned from these mistakes and did their best to improve the software. Their programs are constantly being improved and worked upon. You can make progress on the worst of problems or the best of opportunities. Don't just work out or find a solution for a one-off problem, make the solution methodical and make it repeatable.

From a young age we are taught the unpleasant consequences of making mistakes must be avoided at all cost. The truth is that on your way to success failure is part of the process of succeeding so it cannot be avoided. It can only be avoided by playing it safe the rest of your life and remaining in your comfort zone and not taking any risks at all. The most successful people have met with failure at different levels and they learned from it on their way to success. The people that have failed the most are usually the most successful people. Highly successful people have failed on their way to success. Every failure will teach you and help you to grow, become better and bigger, learn new and vital things and get one step closer to reaching your goals.

The most successful people will tell you the following wisdom from failure. No matter how many times you fail you are not a failure until you decide to give up. Failure is essential on the way to self realisation and success. Failure teaches you resiliency and adjusting your approaches to specific situations. Whenever you embark on a new venture and when you step out of your comfort zone failure becomes inevitable. Successful people have learned the wisdom of failure so they will not judge or laugh at you when you fail because they have been there already and they know the lessons you can learn from failure. Each failure brings you one step closer to achieving your dreams or goals. When you have confronted failure many times the fear of failure often disappears and your confidence increases, you are now willing to attempt big challenges. Each failure makes you better, bigger and stronger. One thing is certain if you have a burning desire to succeed in life, if you want to achieve your dreams, if you want to do something special failure becomes unavoidable.

Steve Jobs deliberately gave weight to the importance of failure when it comes to success when he was referring to the time he was fired from Apple, the company he co-founded. Failure doesn't hurt as much as people would like to think, with the right attitude you have the capability or the art of turning that failure into an exciting and interesting exploration.

Steve Jobs said 'It turned out that getting fired from Apple was the best thing that could have ever happened to me'. He believes that challenge helped him to enter into one of the most creative periods of his life.

It is better to aim at perfection and miss it than to aim at imperfection and hit it. Do not allow the fear of failure to get in your way of achieving the impossible. You cannot allow failure to discourage you but you can learn from it. Go ahead and make mistakes on your way to success. Make all you can because, remember that's where you'll find success on the far side. In hindsight it's not the goods results that make you a stronger, more successful person; it's the failures. This may sound odd, but each failure you have is actually a success.

Thomas Edison had an amazingly positive mental attitude about failure. He said: 'I have not failed I have only found 10000 ways that don't work.' When he was asked why so many of his experiments were failures, he replied by saying that he by no means had a failure in any one of his experiments, instead each experiment gave him any opportunity to discover another way that it would not work and he felt closer to the way it had to work. In reality the only way to success is failing your way to success. You can appreciate victory more after you have failed. Winston Churchill, the former British Prime Minister, said: 'Success is going from failure to failure without losing enthusiasm.'

Failure is the tuition you pay for success. Failure produces positive change and success to those who will not give up or are resilient. You must take charge of your success and dreams. Think of challenges, setbacks, failures and problems as the tuition you have to pay to learn the lessons essential for achieving successful life. This will help you to not react negatively to failure and setbacks, failure has never been pleasant but it is a fact of life. Most successful people will have a story to tell you about their failures before they were successes. Booker T. Washington said: 'I have learned that success is to be measured not so much by the position that one has reached in life as by the obstacles which he has had to overcome while trying to succeed.' Many people who succeed in life did it because they chose to react positively to their failures rather than react negatively. We can draw lessons from successful people – you can make a quantum leap in life by taking advantage of a negative experience and turning it into something positive. Learn from failures, mistakes and setbacks – see as the price you need to pay to succeed.

By taking heed of failure and learn its lessons this will sow seeds of success and eventually you will accomplish your dreams and goals. Never be afraid of taking risk and failing. You learn from what you fail at, and then if you are determined to change it you change that failure into success.

In the words of Soichiro Honda: 'Success is 99 percent failure.' Soichiro Honda started a small workshop in 1938, while he was still in school. His main idea was to develop a piston ring and sell the idea to the Toyota motor Company. He worked day and night developing his idea of a piston ring and often slept in his workshop. He took his wife's jewellery and pawned it for his working capital. Honda finally completed his piston ring and anxiously took a working sample to Toyota. But Toyota told him that the rings did not meet their standards! Instead of giving up his dream and ideas he went back to school where he was ridiculed by the other students. Was this the end of Honda's idea? No, he refused to give up or give in. In the words of Norman Vincent Peale: 'It's always too early to quit.' Rather than focusing and concentrating on his failure, Honda continued working tirelessly towards his goal. Then, after two more years of working hard and redesigning, the breakthrough came when he eventually won a contract with Toyota. Honda would not be denied of his destiny or allow failure to stop him from achieving his goals and dreams. If you are resilient enough you can bounce back from failure and accomplish your dreams and purpose.

Learn Lessons from Failure

Bill Gates said we must take heed of the lessons that failure can teach us. He argues that success can overcast our vision, causing us to become over-confident and unequipped for the new challenges that the future holds. We should not simply discard the patterns of our initial success. We should not be blindfolded by what worked in the past, if it is no longer useful now we should have the courage to embrace new ideas. Gates has always viewed failures as valuable learning lessons. As Windows was gaining popularity, a good number of people were reporting bugs and problems in it and a lot of severe criticism poured in almost every day. Bill Gates took all this in a positive way. These were valuable lessons for him which made him more determined to improve Windows.

Failure is never failure until we accept we have failed. You have to know that failure is only feedback and should be used as a learning curve to help you improve and work on yourself and your ideas. It allows you to be more creative and look for alternative and better ways of doing things.

Napoleon Hill said: 'Every adversity, every failure, every heartache carries with it the seed on an equal or greater benefit.' When you confront failure find out what worked, and what did not work, and map out what you can do differently in the future. The seeds of future success are usually hidden in failure.

Perception is how you look at things. You have the ability and capacity to change the way you see and look at things, so you can change the way you see failure. You can look at failure as life giving feedback to you, and do things in a more intelligent way. On certain occasions life throws you a curveball, knocks you for a loop; when life hands you a lemon, it's an opportunity to make lemonade. The ability to approach failure can be the first step to your success. In the words of Les Brown: 'Just because Fate doesn't deal you the right cards, it doesn't mean you should give up. It just means you have to play the cards you get to their maximum potential' and 'when life knocks you down, try to land on your back. Because if you can look up, you can get up. Let your reason get you back up.' Napoleon Hill said the following about success: 'Before success comes in any man's life, he's sure to meet with much temporary defeat and, perhaps some failures. When defeat overtakes a man, the easiest and the most logical thing to do is to quit. That's exactly what the majority of men do.'

Malcolm Forbes said: 'Failure is success if we can choose to learn from it.' Make a firm decision that you will not quit but that you will be relentless until your temporary failures are swallowed into success. Nothing has the ability and capacity to stop you there is greatness within you.

CHAPTER 14: LEARN FROM YOUR CUSTOMERS

Your most unhappy customers are your greatest source of learning. – Bill Gates

Statistics suggest that when customers complain, business owners and managers ought to get excited about it. The complaining customer represents a huge opportunity for more business. – Zig Ziglar

Anyone who has suddenly and unexpectedly seen the 'blue screen of death' on their Windows™ powered computer understands why Bill Gates has made some of his customers unhappy over the years. The customers that remain silent and don't complain are the ones that don't care enough about the company to come back and buy again. They will vote with their money by just going to someone else that listens. Unhappy customers will help you to work on your ideas, systems and improve. Make sure you listen to your customers concerns at every stage of the process. If you ignore what their concerns, they will soon ignore you.

Listen to your customers and work with them you cannot design in a vacuum and be in touch with people's needs and wants at every stage. Customer needs change with time, listen to all the ideas but filter which ones you take on board. Learning and true innovation comes from strong leadership and the ability to see the best ideas in a world full of ideas.

One thing is clear, you can't solve every customer's problem but you can take it as an opportunity to listen and learn from their problems and focus on improving and designing a better product or service delivery. As a designer you must anticipate problems and work on them. You might not make money in the interim but in the long term you will yield the results of your innovation. Creativity and innovation can thrive in an environment of leadership that rewards in the long term.

You can improve in the way you do things by viewing negative feedback and complaints as a learning opportunity. Many people have been instinctively programmed to react negatively towards feedback and complaints. Janelle Barlow and Claus Moller in their classic business service book titled "A Complaint is a Gift" they said see a complaint as a gift, it means customer expectations were not met. Customer feedback and complaints are actually very important. They give the organisation an opportunity to improve themselves, their products, their services, and also their processes, that is if they act on the feedback they receive.

In this chapter, we'll explore managing complaints and feedback effectively. We'll look at different examples of complaints, and will identify how you can use the closed-loop feedback process to ensure that you learn from the feedback and complaints that you receive.

An effective feedback process gives you the data that you need to create real, lasting improvement. Team morale, product quality, and an organisation's reputation may all improve as a result. A good process helps organisations act on the feedback that they receive. This, in turn, can create a strong bond between the organisation, and its employees and customers.

There are four important steps in a feedback process:

1. Collection of data.
2. Taking action on the data.
3. Communicating the feedback.
4. Refining the changes.

When you take action after feedback, let everyone know. This will show your customers that you really listened, and it will ensure that people continue to offer feedback in the future. This is another important step in the feedback process that is often overlooked.

Studies have revealed that people always complain about issues that truly matter to them and also when they think their complaint will make a difference. When you change your attitude to see your customers complaints as a gift that changes everything. The customers have taken their valuable time to give feedback to the organisation – that is commendable.

The business or the organisation benefit in two ways from customer feedback, in that they get the chance to turn around or improve their experience. Research and surveys have shown that a dissatisfied customer whose problem is fixed or resolved becomes even more loyal to the organisation. The organisation gets the opportunity for valuable feedback of the service that many other customers have experienced but never mentioned to the organisation.

Let me sum up with the following words from Raymond Albert (Ray) Kroc, an American businessman who joined McDonald's in 1954 and built it into the most successful fast food operation in the world: 'If you work just for money, you'll never make it, but if you love what you're doing and you always put the customer first, success will be yours.'

CHAPTER 15: TAKING ACTION TO CREATE RESULTS

You see, in life, lots of people know what to do, but few people actually do what they know. Knowing is not enough! You must take action. – Anthony Robbins

Vision without action is merely a dream. Action without vision just passes the time. Vision with action can change the world. – Joel A. Barker

In order to see results you must take action. In the words of Anthony Robbins: 'many people know what to do to change their lives but it's unfortunate that few people actually action or do what they are supposed to do.' Gates said: 'know how to turn the idea into action.' The problem is not a lack of ideas, they are actually plenty but the problem is execution, turning that idea into reality. In the age of information overload many people have plenty of ideas, even to the extent of overload of ideas. The secret is to take out the ideas that will work and make an impact and change our world. This is an often unmentioned secret of success. Action is the key word. We must have emotional strength in us to take action. As a young boy Bill Gates had nothing to lose. When the odds were against him he still consistently took action by developing more software. This made him a superstar overnight. If not for Bill Gates, Microsoft™ would have not seen the light of day. This was because of his constant delivery of ideas towards his goals and vision.

It's not enough to just dream and believe you must work on your dream by taking action. William Clement Stone said: 'The world is full of dreamers, there aren't enough who will move ahead and begin to take concrete steps to actualise their vision.' You can't just sit down and expect checks coming into your mail box you have to work on your plans. If you want to write a book you must start writing it, do the necessary research and begin the first chapter. It's good to plan, ponder, contemplate, envision and imagine but this must be combined with action. Bill Gates did not simply imagine his dreams of Microsoft but he began to take action by working on his dream. Zig Ziglar, the motivational guru summed it all up when he said: 'It was character that got us out of bed, commitment that moved us into action and discipline that enabled us to follow through.' Many people won't try they give up before trying. Most people think, I can't and just give up before they even get started, even though they really want to increase their income, improve their lives and accomplish more.

You have to apply sustained action, be committed and disciplined in the process of creating the results you want to achieve. When David took on Goliath he had to take action and he was unknown but when he killed Goliath he was headline news in Israel. You can take on your

Goliath too and be in the headlines. Spanish artist Pablo Picasso said: 'Action is the foundational key to all success.' Despite setbacks encountered in the path to success that sometimes come with striving to achieve your goals, believe that success is closer than you think. It is darkest just before dawn, a transformative moment might only be steps away, it could be the next phone call, the next meeting, the next person you meet, the key is to keep moving forward. Henry Ross Perot said: 'Most people give up just when they're about to achieve success. They give up the last minute of the game, one foot away from the winning touchdown.'"

Your thoughts will drive actions and actions create results. Positive, consistent and powerful thoughts are so imperative to success in life and business. Having thoughts that consume you and drive you to take massive action is the piece of the puzzle that many seem to miss out on. You can think and focus on great things coming into your life and on your goals and dreams, but without consistent actions backing those thoughts you will not arrive at the desired destination.

Go and set your big goals, think out those goals and all that you could possibly do to achieve the desired results, and take the massive actions that will bring you success and results. To put it in a simple way taking action creates results. Norman Vincent Peale the American pastor and author said the following: 'Action is a great restorer and builder of confidence. Inaction is not only the result, but the cause, of fear. Perhaps the action you take will be successful; perhaps different action or adjustments will have to follow. But any action is better than no action at all.'

The more you take action from all the great information you've surrounded yourself with the easier it becomes. The more action you take the more positive effects you create. Form a habit of taking action after setting every goal towards achieving that goal. The faster you act, the faster the results come back, the better your next decision is, the more momentum you gain, the quicker success comes, and your motivation to act quickly soars.

Bradley Whitford, an American film and television actor, said: 'Infuse your life with action. Don't wait for it to happen. Make it happen. Make your own future. Make your own hope. Make your own love. And whatever your beliefs, honour your creator, not by passively waiting for grace to come down from upon high, but by doing what you can to make grace happen ... yourself, right now, right down here on Earth.'

You have a choice to act on what you believe. If you don't act why then do you believe. If you believe you can change your life for the better or make a positive mark in your town, village or city or your world, act upon those beliefs. If you think you have a great idea for starting your own business, go ahead and start that business, you must invest your money, time, energy and talents and make that business happen. Bill Gates acted on what he believed and he got the results, go ahead and act on what you believe and you will be amazed with the results – you have the ability to change your world and the world.

Dale Carnegie said the following words: 'Inaction breeds doubt and fear. Action breeds confidence and courage. If you want to conquer fear, do not sit home and think about it. Go out and get busy.' Conrad Hilton the founder of Hilton Hotels said the following: 'Success seems to be connected with action. Successful people keep moving. They make mistakes, but they don't quit.'

Having faith, beliefs and convictions is a great thing, but your life is measured by the actions you take based upon them. You can build a great life and future by doing what you are supposed to do.

Robert Harold Schuller, the founder of the Crystal Cathedral, said: 'High achievers spot rich opportunities swiftly, make big decisions quickly and move into action immediately. Follow these principles and you can make your dreams come true.' You must take action in order to create the results you want the future you want. The power is within you, it's in your hands. Go ahead and make it happen.

CHAPTER 16: LOOK AT THE BIG PICTURE

It's what everyone is after, I mean they want success and when they get it it's an incredible pressure but what you have to do is try to keep the big picture in view. – Gerry Beckley

I do think this next century, hopefully, will be about a more global view. Where you don't just think, 'Yes, my country is doing well', but you think about the world at large. – Bill Gates

Bill Gates understands the principle of looking at the Big Picture. If you look at the Big Picture you will not be destroyed by obstacles in your path. Bill Gates understands that he may be the richest man in the world, but if he doesn't help others lift themselves out of tough circumstances, he has not lived his life to its fullest potential. The Bill and Melinda Gates Foundation is one of the largest donors to disadvantaged people in the world. Gates believes in giving those who are less fortunate. The world is full of people who need help and as long as it is so Gates is not afraid of making more contributions to the society in order to help humanity. He is making history, no one can deny his influence on business and charity, he is working to his fullest potential. Bill is not perfect, but he does care about the choices he makes.

Looking at the big picture simply means the main, most important or major part of something. When you are seeing the big picture you are looking at the situation as a whole rather than just looking at the specific details. In business this principle can be applied in assessing whether an intended project is successful or not, probably by looking at a global scale. This is usually typical with visionaries and world changers, they can quickly see and be able to gauge that the business idea will be successful. Let me use the game of football to illustrate this – a football team winning games and championships is more important than the role played within a team. The goal is more important than the role played. When you look at the big picture in football you are not worried about who scored many goals if you are part of the team. The main goal is to win, so if you can win you have accomplished the big picture.

When you think in terms of the big picture approach you get what I call ripple effect thinking. How does this one action I am taking hurt or help achieve the big picture I have in my head? This will help you to develop the art of projection; a skill that few people have. Many people just do things without really thinking about the future implications of their actions. When people make decisions they don't often look into the future they just look at the event or action itself. Chinese philosopher Xun Zi said: 'In order to properly understand the big picture, everyone should fear becoming mentally clouded and obsessed with one small section of truth.'

Some successful businesses have mastered this art of big picture thinking. They treat each customer like gold, they go above and beyond expectations. This makes the customer do the marketing for the business by telling their friends, relatives and neighbours about the business and they also become a loyal customer.

Big picture thinking does not only apply to business or achieving your goals, it also applies to your everyday life. Every action you take has a ripple effect throughout the world. You shape the lives of those around you, those you will never meet and those you will never know about. Comedienne Ellen DeGeneres said: 'I work really hard at trying to see the big picture and not getting stuck in ego. I believe we're all put on this planet for a purpose, and we all have a different purpose ... When you connect with that love and that compassion, that's when everything unfolds.'

You have to think about the implications of your actions before you act. Get in the habit of looking at the big picture. Are your actions worth it? Form the big picture in your mind and let your life be directed by it. You'll discover that the people who don't think in terms of the future don't have the big picture in their mind. They have no idea of who they want to become and don't know where they want to go, and what they want to achieve. The big picture in your mind is the compass that guides you in the journey of life when you face obstacles. Allow the big picture to be your anchor. When you truly decide to look at the big picture you will achieve your purpose in life, you won't be bogged down by minor details.

CHAPTER 17: GIVE BACK

Give, and it shall be given unto you; good measure, pressed down, and shaken together, and running over, shall men give into your bosom. For with the same measure that ye mete withal it shall be measured to you again. – Luke 6:38

I actually thought that it would be a little confusing during the same period of your life to be in one meeting when you're trying to make money, and then go to another meeting where you're giving it away. – Bill Gates

Giving back to the community is a vital act because it is a reflection of who you really are, your inner person. Most successful people always give to churches and charities, they are not stingy. Are you a giver or a taker? Were you created to give, help and be a blessing to the community or do you expect to just get from the community? Jim Rohn says take 10 percent of your income and give it to the church. Successful people will always be remembered because of their positive contribution to the world.

Make every effort to live out a life that makes a difference in this world; give back more than what you've taken from the community, your life then will then be a true success. Bill Gates did not believe that greed would help in any way at the zenith of his career and he later announced he was going to step down and someone would take over the global company that he founded. It takes great courage and strength to make such a decision. This can positively prove that Bill Gates is a leader of leaders. I recently heard Bill Gates speak at the Milken Institute 2013 Global Conference on Investing in African Prosperity, he talks these days, mainly about his positive vision for raising the health and education standards of poor people around the world. It is in direct contrast to other rich business leaders who tend to concentrate their talk about themselves and their investment portfolios and business success.

Jim Rohn, when he appeared on Mike Litman's show, said 'there is power in giving and tithing'. He said he teaches children about not spending more than 70 cents out of every dollar you earn. The formula is to give away 10 cents to your church or charity, the other 10 cents use as your active capital and the remaining 10 cents keep for passive capital. He said we have to teach generosity while they are still children. Jim Rohn said 10 cents is the start but as you become rich and wealthy you can give more, whatever you think is the best. He said it's about what that money does for you spiritually. Giving is a smart investment and you can also give your time. It will bring returns to you in different ways. It is all worth it for your character, inner spirit and reputation. Giving is a fundamental law of the universe. What you give will always be given back to you multiplied. When a farmer sows corn seeds into the womb of the earth, the seed are incubated and multiplied back to the farmer in the form of harvest. The Book of Life says it all: 'Remember this: The person who plants a little sows sparingly will have a small harvest also reap sparingly, but the person who plants a lot sows generously/bountifully will have a big harvest also reap generously/bountifully' (2 Corinthians 9:6 Expanded Bible).

Bill Gates is now spending his time, effort, energy and money in giving to the community in different projects through his charity, the Bill and Melinda Gates Foundation.

CHAPTER 18: WORK SMART

Wherever smart people work, doors are unlocked. – Steve Wozniak

You have to learn the rules of the game. And then you have to play better than anyone else. – Albert Einstein

If you look into the history of Bill Gates you will realise that he invested numerous hours working on his vision, learning how to write software and programming. Bill Gates is not an overnight success he worked smart and spent more of his time conducting experiments and looking for ways to invent software that would work in a personal computer. His experience with computer programming and coding came through years of trial and error before the Microsoft™ company was even born. Little did they realise that he had substantial experience in programming and had done years and years of hard work before kicking it off. It was this experience which helped him build the first software by Microsoft: MS DOS™. Gates does not believe in the concept of overnight success. Hard work and working smart is what truly counts in the long run.

It was his immense experience in the area of coding and programming that allowed Bill Gates to build the first software, DOS™, that launched Microsoft into its global position. As much as overnight successes are possible, most of the time you have to work hard and smart and invest your time, remember that even the richest man in the world did it through many hours of hard work; and so must you, if you want to see success in your life. Bill Gates has an eye for detail and would, on many occasions, double check everything his company made, so he often re-examined and even rewrote a line of code that he thought wasn't appropriate. Because of his passion for work Microsoft became famous for its quality software. Gates has always argued that nothing can replace hard work. People try shortcuts but all they will get is temporary success, which will soon be wiped out. His leadership mantras and skills were always strong enough to be irresistible and inspirational, so that managers all over the world yearn to learn from his revolutionary ideas.

Steve Job, the co-founder of the Apple Corporation, said: 'Technology is nothing. What's important is that you have a faith in people, that they're basically good and smart, and if you give them tools, they'll do wonderful things with them.'

Bill Gates would choose to employ a lazy person to do a difficult job, because that person will find the easy way to do the job. He will choose to work smart, believing strongly that working smart always produces the best results. Working smart will cut the number of hours put into a project and the job will be done in an efficient manner.

Gates always worked with his business partners like IBM on their terms not his terms. This would put a lot of pressure on his employees because of IBM deadlines. For example when creating MS-DOS software timing was IBM's paramount concern. Microsoft had been given only a few months to work on the project and produce the software. If they had to miss the deadline IBM would have pulled out of the partnership with Microsoft. Microsoft was forced to take a quick shortcut to meet IBM's time limit. They bought the rights to a PC operating system made by another Seattle software company, and built MS-DOS on top of it. This is working smart, creating quality products by building on the foundation of others. Gates later admitted it would have taken a year for Microsoft to create MS-DOS from scratch. Gates motivated his team to persistently to work smart on the project. MS-DOS was eventually finished and delivered on time.

CHAPTER 19: FOLLOW YOUR PASSION

When you set yourself on fire, people love to come and see you burn. – John Wesley

Follow your passion. Nothing – not wealth, success, accolades or fame – is worth spending a lifetime doing things you don't enjoy. – Jonathan Sacks

Passion, intensity and tenacity that is one way to describe Bill Gates. Bill Gates was so passionate about programming to the extent that it kept him motivated about it. He did not work extra hard doing programming because he was motivated by the urge to become a millionaire, it was his passion for programming that pushed him and strengthened him to achieve his goals. He worked very hard because he was simply passionate about what he was doing. Bill Gates found programming software to be extremely interesting and it kept him motivated to go the extra mile. When you follow your passion it will eventually lead you to success. Don't move from opportunity to opportunity trying to find success but focus on what you want for your life and this will eventually lead you to success. Money is everywhere and there are many ways you can make it; the most vital thing is that you follow your passion which leads to success and money will find you naturally.

Money is a very neutral thing. It usually takes the character of the person who has it. Money won't make you happy but people often find this out for themselves, some choose to follow the paper trail rather than their passion. Having money is great, it answers all things – you can buy want you want to enjoy life – but no amount of money will buy fulfilment, satisfaction and time. Our most valuable asset is time and we must spend it wisely.

Some people are in careers that they don't enjoy at all and they is no fulfilment. You only have one life, so don't waste your time working on a career that you hate just because of the money. Are you passionate about the work that you do? There is nothing worse than having to wake up every morning going to a job that you don't enjoy doing. I am not suggesting that you quit your job. You have to use wisdom before you leave that job, you can start by doing what you like to do the most on a part time basis until you are established in your passion and it's rewarding you handsomely enough that you can do it without taking on another job. Your creative process will be boosted and its uniqueness will explode. You are more inclined to come up with creative ideas when you like what you do. When you value money over your passion and health you will find yourself in a cycle of misery that you don't want to be stuck in.

No roadblock will stop you from achieving success when you follow your passion. When you really enjoy what you do, nothing will stop you from getting your work done. Because you are passionate about what you do, you feel unstoppable and nothing can obstruct you from achieving greatness.

Jay Weatherill said: 'You'll be much more successful if you follow your dreams and follow your passions.' Your passion lights up your work, and like a spaceship, it accelerates you past road obstacles that may come in your path. Any impediment that comes your way is obliterated with a creative solution.

A pay cheque may be a means to an end, but a pay cheque is not worth losing your purpose in life. Live the life that you were created for. Don't live by default, live by design. Follow your heart, your purpose. There are no better feelings of achievement than knowing that you accomplished the goals that you set out for yourself. Having the feeling of crossing out the goals you achieved on your list cannot be compared to anything.

Joseph Michael Straczynski, writer and producer, said: 'Follow your passion. The rest will attend to itself. If I can do it, anybody can do it. It's possible. And it's your turn. So go for it. It's never too late to become what you always wanted to be in the first place.' It is always never too late get on the success ladder. You have the ultimate power to decide when to start living your life. You have to be courageous, passionate and brave. Follow your passion and you will surely enjoy it. If you look at almost every famous entrepreneur and research why they got started it wasn't because they wanted to make a lot of money. Successful entrepreneurs start businesses because they have a strong passion for something and want to make a powerful and lasting impact.

When you find out what you are passionate about, what gives you joy, and what drives you to achieve personal success; you have found your own uniqueness and difference. Your uniqueness and difference will not be denied, you will discover your purpose for life and you will be filled with joy in pursuing it.

CHAPTER 20: LEAVE A TRAIL

Don't go where the path may lead, go instead where there is no path … and leave a trail – Ralph Waldo Emerson

In a word I was a pioneer, and therefore had to blaze my own trail. – Major Taylor

In order to become a pioneer you must forget any path you see, make your own path. The path isn't always there. Sometimes you have to make it. Sometimes people will think you are crazy, sometimes you are just ahead of the curve; it's a dream for a reason, and sometimes making your dreams happen takes going out on a limb and giving your all for what you believe in. Bill Gates believed that the personal computer was the future and that there should be one on every desktop and in the living room and it would change the way we work and how we live in unimaginable ways.

You can make a conscious decision to travel the road not taken. In the words of Anthony Robbins: 'A real decision is measured by the fact that you've taken a new action. If there's no action, you haven't truly decided.' You have to make a choice to take the road not travelled and leave a trail. When you do that you are going out of the normal and not settling for the average that everyone else goes for. Forget the path you see, make your own path. When you make your own path and you are successful you become a leader, you are the first and others will follow in your footsteps. Once there is a path people will desire to follow you. When you are always conscious about making your own path you are will recognise opportunities to be different and leave a trail. Felix Baumgartner said: 'If the Wright brothers hadn't put their lives on the line, we would not be flying around the world these days. So we need pioneers.' A pioneer will always travel the road less travelled and they change the world. Alfred Pritchard Sloan, long-time president and chairman of General Motors Corporation, said: 'There has to be this pioneer, the individual who has the courage, the ambition to overcome the obstacles that always develop when one tries to do something worthwhile, especially when it is new and different.' To leave a trail you must never allow yourself to give up, instead you must keep on trying until you pave the way were it seems there is no way. You can win over the obstacles in your path if you have persistent determination. Be resolute, refuse to be intimidated, play to win the game of life.

It is always good to carry a notebook and a pen, as soon as you get an idea or a good thought in your mind write it down. Once your thoughts and ideas are written down they have a lifeline and a chance to live. So many times we lose ideas and thoughts that come to mind, they die before they become productive. Leaving a trail often starts from ideas and thoughts that we work on and develop – you have what it takes to leave a trail of genius. Give your ideas and thoughts a chance to live.

CHAPTER 21: LIVE YOUR VALUES

When your values are clear to you, making decisions becomes easier. – Roy E. Disney

Humanity's greatest advances are not in its discoveries, but in how those discoveries are applied to reduce inequity. – Bill Gates

When you let the world know what you are about, you become a lightening rod and you attract people with the same values. At Microsoft™, Bill Gates attracted people with a passion for changing the world and joining him on a journey to help create better lives through technology and innovation. On the philanthropy side, Gates connects with U2's Bono beyond the music when it comes to sharing their global mission to end poverty, disease and indifference.

Values are guiding standards, or principles of behaviour, which are considered desirable, vital and held in high regard by individuals, organisations and by society. Your values are the things that you believe are important in the way you live and work. Values are essential because they are a statement of who you are and what you believe in, as an individual. When people have lost their values they will not have respect for anyone, even themselves. One thing you should know is, not everyone will agree with your values and this should not affect you, just stand for what you believe in. Your values should determine your priorities and, deep down, they're probably the measures you use to tell if your life is turning out the way you want it to. Let your values guide you in your daily decision making. Your values have to match your decisions. Having values helps you from following selfish ambitions. For example when you value human life you will always want to promote things that protect the sanctity of human life; when you value education you will always strive to promote education.

Steven Harper said: 'I believe very strongly that in this world you have to have values and you have to stand up for your interests and if you don't do those things you're not going to get anywhere.'

When the things that you do, and the way you behave, match your values, life is usually good. When you have strong values you will always work towards fulfilling those values. You have to make a conscious effort to follow your values because they will act as your compass when travelling through the journey of life. Your values will help to fuel your passion. When others are following tradition you can choose to follow a new path. John William Gardner said: 'Our problem is not to find better values but to be faithful to those we profess.'

Bill and Melinda Gates have made their values clear through their charitable Foundation. Their main goal or priority is to reduce hunger and eradicate diseases and extreme poverty, mainly in developing countries. Because they value life and believe everyone has equal value they are working, through their organisation, to promote their values. They simply believe everyone should be given an opportunity to live a healthy life.

CHAPTER 22: SURROUND YOURSELF WITH THE RIGHT PEOPLE

Surround yourself with people who believe in you. – Brian Koslow

You are the average of the five people you spend the most time with. – Jim Rohn

You have to surround yourself with a winning team. Having a team around you with a winning mentality creates synergy. Bill Gates built the best and brightest minds around him and was good at convincing his friends, such as Paul Allen and Steve Ballmer to join him on his adventures. Having bright and smart minds around him created an atmosphere of success. The most important aspect of this is having combined ideas and efforts from smart people improved their chances of innovation. People around Bill Gates also complemented his strengths as well as making up for his weaknesses.

When you surround yourself with the right people they will help you to grow. You have to make a choice of those who can be around you because it is an important decision in life. There is an old proverb that reads: 'If you want to fly with the eagles, don't hang out with the turkeys.' You cannot be successful in life by hanging around people who have no vision. Another old proverb also reads: 'Show me your friends and I'll tell you who you are.' A lot of times we become like the people who surround us, they influence us at some level. People around you either push you up or they are pulling you down. You should surround yourself with people that encourage and support you.

Make a personal inventory of people around you and see whether they are adding value to your life or are taking it away. If you want to be financially successful surround yourself with those who have made it financially. Eventually you will learn their financial habits and they will challenge you. The same thing applies if you hang around with negative people, you will end up being negative. Filter the negative out of your life, it's toxic. Positive people will also make you feel positive; there is always positive energy around them. For example if you want to become a motivational speaker you have to associate yourself with motivational speakers like Zig Ziglar, Jim Rohn, Anthony Robbins and Les Brown. Association, and surrounding yourself with the right people, does not necessarily mean talking to them in person, it could be through their books, speeches, materials and resources. You can even attend motivational speaker seminars.

Eleanor Roosevelt said: 'Great minds discuss ideas; average minds discuss events; small minds discuss people.' People around you will create an environment which will either promote or demote you. Share your dreams and goals with people who value your dreams as much as you do. People who believe in your dreams will add value to you and encourage you to go for your dreams.

There are times that you may feel you want to give up and not follow your dreams this is when you most need people around you who can encourage you and kick start the fire in you. If you are running a company or an organisation you need to recruit people with positive energy who can add value to the organisation and people who can make up for your weaknesses.

An unknown authored quote reads: 'Give thanks to everyone and every opportunity. Life is a blessing. Surround yourself with positive people and make each moment count.'

When you have the right people around you they bring the best out of you. You are assured to achieve your goals. The atmosphere will be charged with success from people who have the same mind and goals.

CHAPTER 23: INNOVATION IS THE HEART AND SOUL OF A BUSINESS

Innovation is the process of turning ideas into manufacturable and marketable form. – Watts Humprey

We are always saying to ourselves, 'We have to innovate. We've got to come up with that breakthrough'. In fact, the way software works, so long as you are using your existing software, you don't pay us anything at all. So we're only paid for breakthroughs. – Bill Gates

The dictionary defines innovation as the act of starting something for the first time or introducing something new. The business dictionary defines innovation as a process of translating an idea or invention into a good or service that creates value for which customers will pay. It's about bringing new ideas to the market and applying research. If you don't innovate you go out of business. The world is always changing and getting even more complex. To stay in the game, or to stay ahead of the game, you have to keep innovating: innovate in your processes, innovate in your products, innovate in the markets, innovate in your service delivery and there are many more areas we can innovate. It does not matter whether it's shaping software or saving the planet to Bill Gates, he always uses innovation to drive impact. In the words of Peter Drucker: 'Innovation is the specific instrument of entrepreneurship. The act that endows resources with a new capacity to create wealth.'

New ideas are developed and converted into useful products and services. In business, innovation often results when ideas are converted by the organisation in order to further satisfy the needs and expectations of their customers. The Japanese use a concept called Kaizen for innovation. Kaizen means continuous improvement or changing for the best. The concept builds into the individual the idea that every worker is responsible for more than maintaining the status quo; part of the job is to suggest small improvements, which could improve efficiency or quality. Build a Kaizen attitude among your people so that they do not just tolerate change but become a part of the process of creating change and innovation. Steve Job, the co-founder of the Apple Corporation, said: 'But innovation comes from people meeting up in the hallways or calling each other at 10:30 at night with a new idea, or because they realised something that shoots holes in how we've been thinking about a problem.'

The Toyota Motor Corporation uses kaizen philosophy; it's one of their core values. No process can ever be declared perfect but it can always be improved. So Kaizen is continuous, constant innovation of the products or services of an organisation. Kaizen in practice means that all team members in all parts of the organisation are continuously looking for ways to improve operations, innovate and people at every level in the company support this process of improvement.

Virtual offices will be the standard of the future, which is a result of innovation. Innovators usually possess a high degree of tenacity. They are relentless, they don't give up. Just as Hannibal said: 'We will either find a way, or make one.' Innovators will always find a way out. For business to survive you have to innovate in the postmodern world, innovation requires a curious mind. Robert Iger said: 'The heart and soul of the company is creativity and innovation.' Bill Gates said: 'I believe in innovation and that the way you get innovation is you fund research and you learn the basic facts.'

CHAPTER 24: MAKING MAXIMUM IMPACT AND CHANGING THE WORLD

The only limit to your impact is your imagination and commitment – Tony Robbins

I was blessed with certain gifts and talents and God gave them to me to be the best person I can be and to have a positive impact on other people. – Bryan Clay

Bill Gates believes in making maximum impact in the world. It is reported there is a little sign on many doors at Microsoft which features a blue monster and reads: 'Change the world, or go home.' His work colleagues testified that Bill Gates has amassed a lot of money in the world, yet he showed up every day to change the world. He could have just retired and enjoyed his money but yet he is energised to make a maximum impact on the world. He fights the good fight to make the world a better place than he found it. Bill Gates joined forces with Warren Buffet, the stock magnate, in a new drive campaigning and encouraging the wealthiest people to give most of their money to philanthropic causes. He's not a seeker of fame or a seeker of fortune, although he has both. He's a maker of maximum impact. Technology is his unique way, and reducing poverty and inequalities in the world is his game. He is at the top of his game and he is also a master of the game of life.

Bill Gates could have retired and enjoyed his billions but he is just as fired up as he was when he founded Microsoft. He is now changing the world and making maximum impact through the Bill and Melinda Gates Foundation. He is on the warpath to eradicate poverty, disease and hunger mainly in the undeveloped world.

You may believe you don't have what it takes to make a difference in the world. You might think it's only reserved for people like Mother Theresa, Thomas Edison, Rosa Parks, Nelson Mandela, Albert Einstein, Bill Gates and Martin Luther King Jr. The truth of the matter is you can still make a difference in the world in your own unique way. You can start in your own small way to make a difference. Mother Teresa said: 'If you can't feed a hundred people, then feed just one.' One thing is clear you already have what it takes to make the world a better place. The size of the contribution does not matter, what is important is the heart to do it. In fact you can start now to make a difference in the world. You can share your love, money, skills, and clothing with the world. Little efforts count. To receive you must give. Let us give love and share happiness with the world and then we will receive more of it.

Sir Richard Branson, business magnate and the founder of Virgin Group, said: 'For a successful entrepreneur it can mean extreme wealth. But with extreme wealth comes extreme responsibility. And the responsibility for me is to invest in creating new businesses, create jobs, employ people, and to put money aside to tackle issues where we can make a difference.'

You can make a long term contribution to people's lives. There is an old proverb that reads: 'If you give a man a fish you feed him for a day. If you teach a man to fish you feed him for a lifetime.' It is better to teach someone how to do something than to do it for them. Giving someone a fish is good for the short term, but it is better to teach them how to do it so that in the long term they can take care of themselves. When you educate them, they will, in turn, provide more value to the world. Go and do something good and change the world. Leave a mark that cannot be erased. Make a difference to the extent that after long you have gone the world will know you have been around.

CHAPTER 25: CONCLUSION

The secrets and lessons of success we can learn from the story of Bill Gates are:

- Success comes with great **vision**. You must have a clear vision for your life that you can relentlessly pursue.

- Success always starts in the mind, with the thoughts you think. Success involves **strategic thinking** – coming up with a clear plan or high level goals to follow.

- You have to **make the most of every opportunity** presented to you. Bill Gates capitalised on the opportunities presented to him and he was successful.

- Go out and **meet people's needs** and you will find your success. When you meet people's needs money and success will eventually follow you. Add **value** to the community and society.

- You must apply the law of **persistence** in pursuit of your goals and dreams. The common element found in the most successful people is persistence. It is the only thing that separates successful people from those who are not successful. Nothing can stand in the path of someone who is persistent. Persistence will always lead to success.

- **Creativity** is an important part of success. You have to learn to think outside the box, be open to new possibilities, use your imagination and come up with new innovative ideas.

- In order to be successful you have to value people and their contribution to the organisation. **Value your employees and customers**, share your vision with your team.

- You must be willing to **learn from failures**. It's good to celebrate success but we must learn from those things that did not work out. There are always seeds of success wrapped up in failures; failure is the price you pay for success.

- You must connect with your customers and **be willing to learn from your customers**. If customers who are not happy use it as an opportunity to learn from them.

- **Taking action creates results**. It's not enough just to dream, you must work on your dreams by taking action. Don't wait for it to happen you must make it happen. Bill Gates did not just dream about Microsoft he acted on his dreams and made it happen and he got the results.

- **Focus on the big picture** as you go ahead to achieve your dream.

- **Give** and it will be given back to you in multiplied measure. Giving is a fundamental law of the universe; you have to apply this law in order to achieve the success you want.

- Don't just work aimlessly you must **work smart and hard**, the results will be success.

- Instead of following the paper trail, **follow your passion** and enjoy what you love to do while you are on your way to success.

- **Leave a trail, be a pioneer**. You have what it takes to leave a trail of genius. In pursuit of whatever you want to achieve be guided by your values so you don't lose track.

- **Be faithful to the values you profess**.

- **Surround yourself with the right people** that will challenge, complement, and support your vision. Make up your mind to be around positive people who can bring the best out of you.

- **Be innovative**. Develop new ideas and covert them into products and services. You have to be continuously innovative to stay in the game.

- Make a difference with maximum impact and **change the world**.

If Bill Gates and others can do it, you can too. There is greatness within you; you will achieve your purpose in life.

BIBLIOGRAPHY

Andrews, Paul. How the Web Was Won: Microsoft from Windows to the Web. New York, Broadway Books, 1999.

Barlow, Janelle and Moller Claus, A Complaint Is a Gift - Using Customer Feedback as a Strategic Tool, San Francisco, CA: Berrett-Koehler Publishers, 1996.

Bennis, W. On becoming a leader. Reading, MA: Addison Wesley Publishing Company, Inc. 1989.

Branson, Richard, Screw It, Let's Do It. Virgin Books, London, 2007

Coelho, Paulo, The Alchemist, New York, HarperCollins Publishers Inc, 1993.

Dearlove, Des, Business the Bill Gates Way: 10 Secrets of the World's Richest Business Leader, Oxford, Capstone Publishing, 1999.

Drucker, Peter, F. Innovation and Entrepreneurship, New York, Harper Business; Reprint Edition, 2006.

Gardner, J. On leadership. New York, The Free Press. 1990.

Gatlin , Jonathan, Bill Gates :The Path to the future, New York, Harper Collins e-books, 1999.

Gates, William, Myhrvold Nathan, and Rinearson Peter. The Road Ahead. New York: Viking Penguin, 1995.

Gates, William, Business @ the Speed of Thought. New York, Warner Books, 1999.

Hancock, T. Guide for vision workshops. Indianapolis, IN: Institute of Action Research for Community Health/Indiana University. 1994.

Hill Napoleon, Think and Grow Rich, Connecticut,The Ralston Society, 1937

Manes, Stephen and Andrews Paul, How Microsoft Mogul Reivented an industry- and Made Him Himself the Richest Man in America, New York, Simon&Schuster, 1994

Maxwell. C. John "Maxwell 2 in 1: Developing the Leader Within You/Developing Leaders Around You." Thomas Nelson Inc, iBooks, 2008.

Meyer, Joyce , Never Give Up! New York, Faith Words Hachette Book Group, 2008.

Nanus, B. Visionary leadership. San Francisco, CA: Jossey-Bass Publishers. 1992.

Rohn, Jim, The Five Major Pieces to the Life Puzzle, Dallas, Jim Rohn Productions, 1991.

Stone, W. Clement, The Success System That Never Fails, New York Pocket, Books, 1989.

Stross, Randall. E., The Microsoft Way, Addison-Wesley, New York, 1996.

Vujicic, Nick. "Unstoppable." The Doubleday Religious Publishing Group, iBooks, 2012.

Wallace, James, and Jim Erickson. Hard Drive: Bill Gates and the Making of the Microsoft Empire. New York: Harper Business, 1992.

Wallace, James. Overdrive: Bill Gates and the Race to Control Cyberspace. New York: John Wiley & Sons, Inc., 1997.

Bill Gates – Biography and History. Online. January 27, 2009. http://inventors.about.com/od/gstartinventors/a/Bill_Gates.htm

http://www.cbn.com/entertainment/Books/700club_myles-munroe.aspx

http://famous.y2u.co.uk/F_Bill_Gates_1.htm

http://www.incomediary.com/top-10-business-lessons-from-bill-gates

http://lifeofexcellence.com/lessons-from-billgates

http://snyderleadership.com/ http://snyderleadership.com/

http://www.youthareawesome.com/finding-ones-passion-working-hard-and-dreaming-big-why-you-can-be-who-you-want-to-be/

http://gigaom.com/2012/04/22/apple-vs-google-lessons-from-bill-gates-playbook/

http://www.businessdictionary.com/definition/creative.html#ixzz2k3mRjAcA

http://www.ziglar.com/quotes

http://www.ziglar.com/quotes/if-you-want-reach-goal

http://www.ziglar.com/quotes/zig-ziglar/you-were-born-win-be-winner

http://www.neve-family.com/books/tozer/neglect/30.html

http://www.success.com/article/zig-ziglar-defining-success#sthash.cSTHN0Qk.dpuf

http://www.the-star.co.ke/news/article-113031/success-all-starts-mind#sthash.MTsL77K9.dpuf

http://ezinearticles.com/?Christian-Wisdom-Book-Review---The-Double-Diamond-Principle&id=7177228

http://www.forbes.com/sites/mfonobongnsehe/2013/02/24/five-lessons-from-zimbabwes-richest-man-strive-masiyiwa/

http://www.evancarmichael.com/Work-Life/1783/How-Persistent-are-You.html

http://danache.com/chinese-bamboo-tree-story/

http://www.articlesbase.com/entrepreneurship-articles/colonel-sanders-story-of-perseverance-entrepreneurship-100394.html

http://jackcanfield.com/what-stops-you-from-taking-action/#sthash.ZlZzHjj0.dpuf

http://www.sacred-texts.com/nth/tsoa/tsoa18.htm

http://www.mindtools.com/pages/article/newTED_85.htm#sthash.dUuDm9h5.dpuf

http://www.businessdictionary.com/definition/creative.html#ixzz2k3mRjAcA

http://abcnews.go.com/Technology/steve-jobs-fire-company/story?id=14683754&page=2

http://www.success.com/blog/chapter-two-the-nine-ps-of-winning#sthash.9vlFwQAi.dpuf

http://jimrohn.com/

http://EzineArticles.com/5920554

http://www.youtube.com/watch?v=UmCtWskzmAQ

http://www.youtube.com/watch?v=hNZli6CQECk

http://www.youtube.com/watch?v=Ey9nBHCUO-g

Motivational quotes not attributed in the bibliography above have been obtained from reputable quotes sources such as the websites Goodreads, Brainy Quotes, Famous quotes and Search quotes.

ABOUT THE AUTHOR

Dr Lyton Chandomba is an accomplished motivator, speaker, author and leadership development consultant. He is appreciated by countless people for his ability to encourage and inspire people. He is the founder and president of Leadershift Factory and Raising Champions. He is involved in mentoring and coaching people. His mandate is to Raise Champions.

Printed in Poland
by Amazon Fulfillment
Poland Sp. z o.o., Wrocław

55985051R00070